THE BIRTH OF TORNADO

ROYAL AIR FORCE HISTORICAL SOCIETY

The opinions expressed in this publication are those of the contributors concerned and are not necessarily those held by the Royal Air Force Historical Society.

Copyright 2002: Royal Air Force Historical Society

First published in the UK in 2002 by the Royal Air Force Historical Society

All rights reserved. No part of this book may be reproduced or transmitted in any form or by any means, electronic or mechanical including photocopying, recording or by any information storage and retrieval system, without permission from the Publisher in writing.

ISBN 0-9530345-0-X

Typeset by Creative Associates
115 Magdalen Road
Oxford
OX4 1RS

Printed by Advance Book Printing
Unit 9 Northmoor Park
Church Road
Mothmoor
OX29 5UH

CONTENTS

Welcome by Society Chairman – AVM Baldwin	7
Introduction by Air Chf Mshl Sir Anthony Skingsley	8
Eroding The Requirement by Gp Capt John Heron	10
Air Staff Studies And Political Background by Anthony S Bennell	13
Evolution Of The Tornado Project by Dr William Stewart	23
Tornado/MRCA - Establishing Collaborative Partnerships And Airframe Technology by Gerrie Willox	31
RB 199 – The Engine For Tornado by Dr Gordon Lewis	50
Tornado IDS Avionic System by Peter Hearne	56
The Munich Scene by Alan Thornber	65
Development Flying by Paul Millett	84
Into Service - Training & Operations by AVM R P O'Brien	100
Conclusions - Industry by John Wragg	113
Conclusions - Procurement Organisation by Dr William Stewart	116
Conclusions - An RAF Viewpoint by AVM R P O'Brien	118
<div align="center">Discussion</div>	120
Chairman's Closing Remarks by Air Chf Mshl Sir Anthony Skingsley	129

Supplementary Papers

A Footnote – Could A Developed Buccaneer Have Filled The Bill? by Peter Hearne	130
Observations From The OR Coalface by Gp Capt John Heron	133
Air Density Measurement Transducers For Tornado by Talbot K Green	138
Calibration Of Pressure Sensors by Robin J Baker	139

Note. *As is often the case in reporting the proceedings of a seminar, in the interests of clarity, cogency and overall coherence, some editorial discretion has been exercised in the presentation of some papers. Where this has occurred, the changes have in no way altered the sense of the original content.* **Ed**

ROYAL AIR FORCE HISTORICAL SOCIETY

President	Marshal of the Royal Air Force Sir Michael Beetham GCB CBE DFC AFC
Vice-President	Air Marshal Sir Frederick Sowrey KCB CBE AFC

Committee

Chairman	Air Vice-Marshal N B Baldwin CB CBE FRAeS
Vice-Chairman	Group Captain J D Heron OBE
Secretary	Group Captain K J Dearman
Membership Secretary	Dr Jack Dunham PhD CPsychol AMRAeS
Treasurer	John Boyes TD CA
Members	Air Commodore H A Probert MBE MA
	* J S Cox Esq BA MA
	* Dr M A Fopp MA FMA FIMgt
	* Group Captain P Gray BSc LLB MPhil MIMgt RAF
	* Wing Commander C McDermott RAF
	Wing Commander C Cummings
Editor, Publications	Wing Commander C G Jefford MBE BA
	* *Ex Officio*

ABBREVIATIONS

Note. When Strike Command was established in 1968, the word 'strike' had meant merely to deliver a blow. By the late-1970s, however, British (but not NATO) military *patois* tended to associate the adjective 'strike' with nuclear operations, as distinct from 'attack' which implied the delivery of conventional weapons; if it was necessary to make the point, a dual-capable unit would be described as a strike/attack squadron. Although it was not recognised universally, this convention remained in use thereafter within those elements of the community where such distinctions were of significance, and it is reflected in some of the following presentations. It has presumably become redundant within the RAF now that the Service no longer has a nuclear capability.

ACE	Allied Command Europe
ADV	Air Defence Variant (of the Tornado)
AFVG	Anglo-French Variable Geometry (project)
APU	Auxiliary Power Unit
ATE	Automatic Test Equipment
BAC	British Aircraft Corporation
BITE	Built-In Test Equipment
CCIP	Continuously Computed Impact Point
CFE	Central Fighter Establishment
CSAS	Command and Stability Augmentation System
ECM	Electronic Counter Measures
ECS	Environmental Control System
EPU	Emergency Power Unit
ESG	*Electronik Systems Gruppe*
ESAMS	Elliotts Space Advanced Military Systems
EW	Electronic Warfare
FBW	Fly-By-Wire
FCS	Flight Control System
FLIR	Forward Looking Infra Red
GAF	German Air Force
GFE	Government Furnished Equipment
GPS	Global Positioning System
HAS	Hardened Aircraft Shelter
HUD	Head Up Display
IDS	InterDictor Strike

IFF	Identification Friend of Foe
IFR	In-Flight Refuelling
IMO	Interim Management Organisation
IN	Inertial Navigation
IOC	Initial Operational Capability
JOTSC	Joint Operational Training Study Committee
JSF	Joint Strike Fighter
JWG	Joint Working Group
LCN	Load Classification Number (a measure of runway strength)
LLTV	Low Light Television
MB	Messerschmitt-Bölkow
MBB	Messerschmitt-Bölkow-Blohm
MOU	Memorandum of Understanding
MRCA	Multi-Role Combat Aircraft
MTBF	Mean Time Between Failures
MTU	*Motoren und Turbinen-Union*
NAMMA	NATO MRCA Management Agency
NAMMO	NATO MRCA Management Organisation
NKF	*Neuen Kampflugzeug*
OCAMS	On board Check out And Monitoring System
OCU	Operational Conversion Unit
OR	Operational Requirements (Branch of MOD)
ORBAT	**Or**der of **Bat**tle
QCP	E**Q**uipment **C**ontrol **P**anel
QRA	Quick Reaction Alert
R&D	Research and Development
RWR	Radar Warning Receiver
SACEUR	Supreme Allied Commander Europe
SAHRS	Standard Attitude and Heading Reference System
SE	System Engineering
TACEVAL	**Tac**tical **Eval**uation
TFR	Terrain Following Radar
TIALD	Thermal Imaging Airborne Laser Designator
TSC	Tornado Steering Committee
TTTE	Tri-National Tornado Training Establishment
TU	Turbo-Union Ltd
TWCU	Tornado Weapons Conversion Unit
WCU	Weapons Conversion Unit

THE BIRTH OF TORNADO
BAWA, FILTON, 24th OCTOBER 2001
WELCOME ADDRESS BY THE SOCIETY'S CHAIRMAN
Air Vice-Marshal Nigel Baldwin CB CBE FRAeS

Ladies and Gentlemen.

It is a pleasure to welcome you all. Before I introduce our Chairman for the day, I would like to thank, on all our behalves, Rolls-Royce and British Aerospace who have generously sponsored the day, thus helping us to keep the costs to our members down. A particular thank you goes to George Brown, the Chairman of the BAWA - the Bristol Aerospace Welfare Association — and to Alex Clarke and their team for their hospitality and their work in setting up the day. I also include in my thanks Gp Capt Jock Heron, my Vice-Chairman, who has done most of the persuading, cajoling and worrying that is needed to make such a day possible. Many of you will have been here four-and-a-half years ago when we looked at the 'TSR2 With Hindsight', and will have the journal recording that day on your bookshelves. That was one of the highlights of the Society's fifteen-year career. We hope to build on that today, not least in recording the event, so that this too will result in another excellent hardback journal.

Our Chairman for the day, Air Chf Mshl Sir Anthony Skingsley, had more to do with the emerging MRCA/Tornado than most. In 1968-71, as a wing commander, he held a critically important post within the Operational Requirements Branch in Whitehall's Air Force Department; he was the MOD's Director of Air Plans during the Tornado's development phase in the late 1970s and in the late 1980s, just prior to the Gulf War, he was CinC RAF Germany with Tornados based at Brüggen and Laarbruch.

Sir Anthony, the Society is delighted that you accepted the challenge of keeping this day on track. You have control.

INTRODUCTION BY SEMINAR CHAIRMAN
Air Chief Marshal Sir Anthony Skingsley GBE KCB MA

Chairman, Ladies & Gentlemen. Good morning.

I don't yet know how big a challenge this seminar is going to be but I shall doubtless find out in the course of the day. Let me first thank you all for coming and express my personal thanks to Jock, because he has done all the actual preparation for today's gathering, including preparing for me all things that I need to have to hand as Chairman, so many thanks for that Jock.

Today we are going to focus on the Tornado and its early development. In my judgement, the Tornado is one of the most important aeroplanes we have had since the war. It certainly ranks with the Hunter and the Canberra, because it gave us, for the very first time, something we had been looking for ever since 1945, the ability to do attack missions by night and in bad weather. The Tornado gave us that capability which we have now had for the last two decades. It was therefore, a successful project and, as your Chairman mentioned, I had seven squadrons of these beasts in my command in Germany, I flew regularly with the crews and I can assure you they loved the aeroplane. They knew they had the best aircraft of its type in the world and they were very content with it.

Today we are going to look at the genesis of the project and the programme falls naturally into two parts, divided by lunch! In the morning, we shall look at the political background governing the acquisition of the aeroplane; what the Air Force Department was looking for; what MinTech was looking for (remembering that in those days it was a separate Ministry); and what industry was trying to achieve within all of this. In the afternoon, we shall look at the development of the aeroplane itself and its initial introduction into service. I had better perhaps also make clear what we are not going to do. We are not going to look at the fighter version because, in the time available, that would, I think, be biting off more than we could chew in one day. So I am going to rule the F.3 out of court and I shall have to rule offside any attempts to get into discussion on the fighter. Similarly, we shall not address the fairly recent update to the strike/attack version to produce the current GR Mk 4. Our business is to examine how the project started.

I think we can fairly claim that our speakers are all experts in their field, with first hand knowledge of the project, and we should have a very interesting day ahead of us.

If I might just address our speakers for a moment, to stress the point that, in order to get through the day, it is very important that we keep to our allocated time slots. I shall, therefore, set a good example by stopping well within my assigned 10 minutes and move on to introduce Gp Capt Jock Heron, who once worked for me in OR13.....

ERODING THE REQUIREMENT
Group Captain Jock Heron

Commissioned from Cranwell in 1957, Jock Heron flew Hunters followed by a stint with the CFE and an exchange tour with the USAF on the F-105. By 1967 he was at the MOD where he helped to draft AST392, the specification for the MRCA. He then joined the Harrier world before commanding West Drayton and Port Stanley; his last RAF appointment was with the air staff at High Wycombe. He spent the next ten years with Rolls-Royce as the Company's Military Affairs Executive before his final retirement in 1998. He is Vice-Chairman of our Society.

The operational requirement for the weapons system which became the Tornado was, not surprisingly, complicated by national politics, MOD manoeuvring, money, or more accurately a lack of it, and industrial aspirations but it will be helpful to remind ourselves of the several projects which, during the ten years before its conception, were an influence on the aircraft which today is the core of the offensive front line of the Royal Air Force.

By the late 1950s it was recognised that the V-bomber Force with its 1,500 mile radius of action at high level was likely to become increasingly vulnerable to surface-to-air missiles and the requirement emerged for a low altitude, all-weather strike/attack aircraft which would be able to penetrate at high speed below enemy early warning and fire control radar systems. The aircraft would complement the V-bomber strategic platforms for a time before ultimately replacing them as the UK's principal manned aircraft nuclear weapons system. The subsequent demise of the Blue Streak and Skybolt missile systems and the adoption of the submarine launched Polaris strategic missile did not eliminate the need for a complementary tactical strike/attack aircraft, a role which the obsolescent Canberra fulfilled at that time.

Other nations were developing a variety of fighter aircraft to meet the need for an all-weather low level tactical nuclear bomber. The American F-105D, the French Mirage IIIE and the widely used F-104G all entered service in the 1960s but their radius of action was limited; they needed long runways and substantial airfield infrastructure to support their operation and they were incapable of blind attack with conventional weapons. In the late 1950s a number of similar British projects was being developed to meet the forecast need to replace the Canberra, such as the Hawker P1121. However it was cancelled along with many other manned aircraft projects in 1957 following the infamous Sandys Defence White Paper but the basic requirement for the Canberra replacement was preserved and was to emerge subsequently as the TSR2, a hugely ambitious project which had a radius of action of 1,000 miles with six 1000 lbs bombs, or a nuclear weapon, carried internally and the ability to operate from austere bases with short runways and limited ground support. At the same time the Royal Navy planned to embark the Buccaneer as its principal strike/attack aircraft with a potential radius of action of over 450 miles with a nuclear weapon or four 1000lbs bombs carried internally although it too was incapable of blind attack over land with conventional weapons.

Cancellation of the TSR2 in 1965 caused consternation both within industry and the Royal Air Force but the new Labour government still recognised the requirement for such a capability. It was agreed that limited numbers of a modified F-111 which had no conventional bomb bay but had a similar radius of action to the TSR2 would be acquired and that a larger number of the smaller BAC/Dassault Anglo-French Variable Geometry (AFVG) strike/attack aircraft with a 600 mile radius of action but no internal weapons carriage would complement the F-111 force within the RAF. Regrettably the French withdrew from the AFVG agreement in June 1967 and six months later the F-111 was cancelled by the Labour government. By January 1968, despite an order for a number of Buccaneers, the long term future looked bleak with plans for the RAF strike/attack front line in disarray.

So what were the options to replace the Canberra? National work embraced a study of a UKVG aircraft, based on the AFVG which, with external fuel, would have had a radius of action of 650 miles at low level and a variant of the Buccaneer, the 2*, which had an improved radius of action, the ability to operate from runways with a lower LCN and an enhanced avionics suite. The MOD was exposed to foreign industry's attempts to promote a variety of paper projects such as a Mirage IV powered by twin Speys, a similarly powered twin Viggen, the US FX, which became the F-15, and the Northrop P530/P600 which, five years later, was developed into the F/A-18. Meanwhile the French had gone on to build the swing-wing Mirage G, three examples of which were flown on extensive trials. The type did not enter service but it too was promoted as a candidate to meet the UK requirement.

Eventually as we prepared for our first meeting in July 1968 in Munich with our military counterparts in the F-104 consortium we were directed to state our requirement for a surprisingly modest 450 mile radius of action, with external fuel, and, if necessary to compromise below that figure, to as low as 400 miles. The notional mission, which was to size the aircraft, demanded a radius of action of 250 miles without external fuel while carrying four 1000 lbs bombs. With two underwing fuel tanks the requirement was a radius of action of 400 miles with an external load of four 1000 lbs bombs and two undefined stores on the outboard pylons. The sortie profile included a take off roll of not more than 2500 ft, cruise at best range speed at low level to an acceleration point to enable final penetration to the target at M0.9 for 150 miles, jettisoning the external tanks when empty, spend two minutes in the target area at full power, egress at M0.9 for 150 miles, return to base for the remainder at best range speed with sufficient fuel reserves and to land within a ground roll of 1500 ft.

So from the Vulcan's 1500 mile radius of action at high level we had reduced to 1000 miles at low level for the TSR2 and F-111, to 600 miles with external fuel for the AFVG and finally to 400 miles, also with external fuel, for the MRCA. It seemed that expediency ruled as we entered the negotiations!

AIR STAFF STUDIES AND POLITICAL BACKGROUND
Anthony S Bennell

Tony Bennell is a retired Assistant Secretary in the Air Force Department and a former member of the Air Historical Branch where he prepared a study of 'Defence Policy and the Royal Air Force 1964-1970', a period of particular relevance to this seminar. He has also been a Research Associate at the International Institute for Strategic Studies and a Director of the Royal Asiatic Society. He is a fellow of the Royal Historical Society.

In covering the period from July 1967 to October 1968, I shall explore two related themes. The first concerns the air staff requirements of a number of NATO nations which, for Britain, Germany and Italy, eventually led to the Tornado specification. The second theme addresses the political background against which the specification evolved and against which HMG ultimately agreed to British participation in a collaborative project.

When the Anglo-French Variable Geometry project collapsed in July 1967, a decision was required as to whether design work should be continued at Warton, the possible need for such a fall-back position having actually been under consideration since 1966. Ministers were therefore already aware of the scale of effort that would be involved if the project were to become a solely British venture. Nevertheless, following the French withdrawal, ministers called for 'a wide-ranging interdepartmental examination (*into*) the military requirement for combat aircraft beyond the mid-1970s, the advantages and disadvantages of retaining a capability in this country to design, develop and produce advanced military aircraft, and the consequences for the aircraft industry if this capability was not retained.'

These terms of reference indicated very real collective Cabinet reservations over the proposition that it would be appropriate to embark on a British-only research and development project. There were two causes of concern. First, should it become necessary to devalue the pound, either in the context of an attempt to join the European Community or otherwise, a drastic review of government expenditure, including defence, would be inevitable. Such a review (it would be the sixth since October 1964) would have a considerable negative impact on both the annual research and development budget and on the overall defence budget, which was normally projected over a ten-year period.

Secondly, there was uncertainty over global defence policy. In the context of force deployments, the resolve reflected in the July 1967 White Paper was more apparent than real. In many respects the Cabinet was actually split and the balance of opinion, which was then opposed to an accelerated withdrawal from the Far and Middle East, could well have been reversed.

One solution to the problem of re-equipping the RAF's front line would be to replace the moribund AFVG with another collaborative project, for which there were several potential partners. For instance, having received a presentation on the operational capabilities of the AFVG earlier in the year, in July 1967 Bonn indicated that the FRG might be prepared to replace France in such a programme. There was some optimism that wider support might be found within NATO if the operational requirements of the F-104 Replacement Group (Germany, Italy, Canada, Belgium and the Netherlands) could be reconciled with the British proposals, which seemed likely.

As Secretary of State, Healey agreed to a formal approach being made to Bonn with the proviso that 'we should make it clear to BAC that the Government will regard the European or NATO requirement as having a higher priority than a military requirement outside Europe, and those engaged on the project study should be guided by this in considering any elements in the performance parameters which may have to be degraded.' At the time the German aircraft industry was handling only maintenance contracts for aircraft built elsewhere. Nevertheless, despite its lack of development or production experience, it was collaborating with the United States in the definition of a possible replacement for both the G.91 and the F-104 and the German air staff was attempting to lead the drafting of the requirement for a new operational aircraft to satisfy the needs of the F-104 Replacement Group.

While it was in Bonn in July 1967 the British delegation's views were sought on collaboration with the USA. It responded somewhat guardedly, Healey's Chief Adviser Projects stating that 'while we would not rule it out, we did not want to become subcontractors in the United States aircraft industry, and......would prefer bilateral collaboration so as to retain a military aircraft design capability.'

At much the same time, CAS informed the Secretary of State that there was still a requirement for the type of attack and reconnaissance aircraft that had been represented by the AFVG. CAS suggested that a number of possible scenarios, involving a variety of political and military situations, should be studied. Each exercise would evaluate the capabilities of the various types of aircraft that were potentially available and assess their ability to satisfy the operational imperatives.

Healey was not prepared to endorse the study as proposed, since he considered that its scope should not be limited solely to the issue of the next attack/reconnaissance aircraft and, furthermore, that it should not be taken for granted that additional attack and reconnaissance capacity would be required over and above that represented by the prospective F-111s. He believed that the enquiry should focus on the changing requirements of NATO, in the light of a current review of strategy, following the adoption of a policy of flexible response in May 1967 and the circulation of SACEUR's Special Study to member states in August. In short, Healey wanted the study to determine whether an aircraft could be built which would 'cater, both operationally and financially, for the needs of our European allies.'

Nevertheless, the fact remained that the demise of the AFVG had left a gap in the projected front line and CAS maintained that, unless it was filled, British forces would be unable to operate in a hostile air defence environment. Starting from the premise that Britain should sustain its capacity to design and produce advanced military aircraft, CAS recommended that the design of a variable geometry aircraft should be undertaken as a national project with collaborative partners being invited to join the enterprise at a later date. As a first step, he advocated the granting of interim authority for BAC to continue the design studies that were already in train at Warton, but now on a purely national basis.

The other Chiefs of Staff associated themselves with CAS's position and expressed the view that, without an adequate strike and reconnaissance capability, it would not be possible to undertake the extensive commitments set out in the draft July 1967 White Paper. These commitments included (apart from continued participation in European defence) maintaining a presence in the Far East and Persian Gulf until the mid-1970s. CDS proposed that a study, very similar to that recently suggested by CAS but vetoed by the Secretary of State, be undertaken within the MOD to confirm the requirement for the proposed aircraft. As before, it was to consider a variety of potential scenarios, operational situations and political assumptions. As before, Healey had his reservations, noting that the enquiry would need to take account of the 'political climate in which my colleagues and I are likely to consider specific issues relating to our long-term military capacity outside Europe.' He did not 'regard the scenarios as more than general criteria relevant to possible contingencies, by which to evaluate our military aircraft requirements and alternative ways of meeting them.' The potential requirement would also require careful evaluation within the NATO context. 'This is the area of study in which it will be of crucial importance to establish if there is a valid requirement for a new strike/reconnaissance aircraft in the 1970s, and if so its precise character, taking into account not only the strategic case which we have been arguing in NATO but also such factors as the potential role of missiles in the longer term.'

The extended statement of the operational tasks required of a new combat aircraft in the mid-1970s included strategic reconnaissance to a depth of 500 miles into enemy territory, tactical reconnaissance over the battle area and to a depth of 100 miles, attack capability to a depth of 300 miles into enemy territory, for counter-air, counter-missile and interdiction targets, and a maritime strike range of 800 miles if (in the NATO context) bases in Norway were available, and 1200 miles if not. Tasking outside the NATO area would require similar capabilities.

Meanwhile other options were being put forward, including delaying a start on the specification and design of an aircraft. The air staff briefed against this, although Healey saw some advantage in postponing the early replacement of the V-bombers, then expected to be progressively withdrawn from service during the early 1970s. Extending the timeframe in this way would, he argued, permit the design and development of an aircraft of better performance and of lower cost, which would enhance its sales prospects, and provide the opportunity to harmonise British and German operational requirements. He proposed that his ministerial colleagues' recent remit for a 'wide-ranging interdepartmental examination' should be met by MOD studies which had confirmed the requirement for another generation of manned aircraft, although changes in NATO strategy and the need to work with the Germans meant that further work would have to be done on specifications. The aim, Healey said, should be 'to get a contingent decision from Ministers that we should go ahead with a new aircraft project, the precise role and detailed performance of which would have to be left open until it was known whether the German government would join.' It was accepted that this would involve an appreciable delay in the initiation of the project, at least into early 1968.

Briefing within the air staff had noted Healey's unwillingness to consider military contingencies outside Europe or to commit himself to a new strike/reconnaissance aircraft, even if the Germans did appear to be willing to collaborate. A revised analysis scheme, eventually to emerge as the Future Combat Aircraft Study, was now devised to consider: the effectiveness of both strike and reconnaissance operations; the effect of technical developments on the air defence environment within the Central Region; the extent to which tactical reconnaissance aircraft might be displaced by satellites; and the future role of V/STOL in close support operations. This approach was endorsed at a ministerial meeting chaired by Healey, which noted that the timescale of this extended enquiry (it was not expected to report in mid-1968) fitted well with the anticipated delays that the Germans might encounter in reaching a decision on a new aircraft.

By this time, November 1967, there was more information available on the positions of the prospective collaborative partners. In mid-October, a meeting of the Chiefs of Air Staff of the F-104 Replacement Group had rejected a draft operational requirement as being too complex and too expensive. The British air staff was now invited by the Replacement Group to give a presentation on their assessment of the operational requirement. This presentation emphasised the findings of the extensive background studies that had been carried out into the basis for the requirement, these findings being reflected in the current draft.

The British solution was a twin-engined aircraft with a two-man crew. The unit cost projected by the Ministry of Technology was £1.55M on a run of 300. The initial reaction of the Replacement Group members was largely confined to discussing of the depth of strike and reconnaissance missions and on the impact that this might have on the avionics fit.

This attempt to launch a collaborative venture was being made against a depressing British economic background. Reference has already been made to the possibility of a devaluation of sterling and in November 1967 the attempt to maintain parity had to be abandoned. Devaluation would clearly have to involve economy measures and the government soon embarked on the inevitable review of public expenditure. In the context of defence, there were two major decisions. First, British forces were to be withdrawn from the Far East and Middle East by the end of 1971. Secondly, the F-111 contract was cancelled.

In the meantime, in December, Healey had sought to take the collaborative venture further with Schroeder, the German Minister of Defence, but it was clear that German thinking was still too vague to make worthwhile discussions possible. More depressingly, however, it was evident that there was a strong lobby in Bonn which believed that it would be possible, and advantageous, to exclude both the French and the British aircraft industries from the design, development and production of an aircraft for the German Air Force. Further discussions with the German authorities, shortly before the F-111 order was cancelled, led to their reluctant agreement to consider, in conjunction with Britain, the requirement for a light strike aircraft. This activity was endorsed at ministerial level 'even if this was only to gain further knowledge of their thinking.'

The cancellation of the F-111 inevitably focused attention on the long-term problem of re-equipping the RAF's front line and in February 1968 CAS returned to the possibility of a British-designed aircraft to meet a British operational requirement. If collaboration was deemed to be essential, however, he did not see why this necessarily had to be with Germany, as a derivative of the Mirage G might serve just as well. Healey's response was to warn that it could not be assumed that current levels of defence expenditure were sacrosanct and he suspected that the premium attached to a purely national project would make it unaffordable. Indeed, he stated that he had already formed the provisional view that 'some form of collaboration is likely to be the only solution.' The choice boiled down to a collaborative project or abandoning a national design capability altogether. To tide them over, pending a decision, it was suggested that the BAC team at Warton should be authorised to carry out an eighteen-month study. The Treasury agreed to fund the work, but only until June 1968.

By April 1968 the F-104 Replacement Group had agreed to provide details of their proposed specification, provided that the British declared a specific numerical interest in a joint aircraft. The range and payload parameters of the projected aircraft were fairly close to those which were expected to emerge from the still incomplete Future Combat Aircraft Study. On the other hand, the proposed avionics fit appeared to be inadequate and it was considered that the forecast of maximum unit cost was too low. At a meeting of the Replacement Group held in Rome in May 1968, to which the UK had been invited, the British presentation outlined the sort of management scheme, both governmental and industrial, which would be needed to control a major and complex interdependent project.

As the point at which it would become necessary to sign a Memorandum of Understanding drew nearer, Healey put the matter to his ministerial colleagues. He pointed out that the Future Combat Aircraft Study would confirm the requirement for the RAF to have a new attack/reconnaissance aircraft. The specification for this aircraft was sufficiently close to that being considered by the possible consortium for there to be a real prospect of a collaborative venture. To hold back at this point would be to 'forfeit an excellent opportunity of broadening the basis of European collaboration in advanced technology and defence procurement,' although the organisational details of such an arrangement had yet to be worked out. The Treasury had reservations over the implications of such a complex international project and advocated a straightforward offshore purchase or manufacture under licence. The Treasury further advised against entering into any formal commitment, such as that involved in a Memorandum of Understanding, until the findings of the Future Combat Aircraft Study had been published. By stressing the limited nature of both the initial commitment and of expenditure to the end of 1968, however, Healey secured the endorsement he sought, although warnings were still being sounded over the risks inherent in making *any* commitment to a major project with a long timescale.

Despite earlier attempts by the Replacement Group to promote a more binding and long-term obligation, the Memorandum of Understanding that was eventually signed in Bonn on 17 July 1968 was a relatively simple affair addressing only the initial stages of the project. The signatories were the British, Germans, Italians and Dutch, the Canadians and Belgians withdrawing from the collaborative venture at this stage, although they retained the right to be associated with it for a further period. The agreement provided for the conduct of 'parametric studies' to determine the operational characteristics of the proposed aircraft and included a compromise statement of intention over the future form of contractual arrangements.

The UK's very comprehensive Future Combat Aircraft Study was completed in July 1968. Nothing comparable had been attempted by the other members of the consortium. It was particularly notable that the British exercise had considered the whole NATO area, including the flanks and adjacent waters, whereas the work undertaken by the Replacement Group had been concerned only with the Central Region. As expected, the study confirmed the requirement for a credible long range attack capability, for both deterrent and operational purposes, and, while recognising the increasing significance of satellite reconnaissance, it also confirmed a continuing need for the flexibility conferred by manned tactical reconnaissance aircraft. The study also conclusively demonstrated that the aircraft needed to be able to operate at high speed at very low level and to possess a truly all-weather capability.

This was convincing enough for the UK but, as Healey was reminded at this stage, 'the Germans and the British require the aircraft for essentially different tasks. The British want the capability for counter-air and interdiction operations with both conventional and nuclear weapons. The Germans want a capability with nuclear weapons only.' It followed that the British payload and range requirements were more demanding than those of the consortium. While compromise might be possible, it could be achieved only by foregoing some part of the capability for NATO flank and maritime tasking, or by accepting exclusively continental basing of British owned versions of the aircraft, or by accepting limitations on the offensive tasking area.

Presentations setting out these issues took place in September 1968. A range of costed options was examined, making it possible to assess, for example, the extra cost to the Germans of the unique British operational requirements, and of those of the Germans to the British. There was some prospect that these gaps could be closed and the major difficulty now became one of industrial organisation rather than the reconciliation of operational requirements.

An examination of briefs prepared for the Secretary of State during October 1968, reveals the pressures on the project at this stage. CAS was clearly concerned that key performance characteristics specifically required by the RAF were being excessively degraded in the interests of securing a collaborative project. He also feared that if the costs of the projected joint aircraft increased this would be compensated for by further pruning of the specification at the expense of the NATO flanks and the maritime case. Furthermore, any compromises on issues of range and payload could necessitate a tanker purchase which would negate the savings that could follow from collaboration. Once again, CAS urged either a bilateral arrangement with the French or the Americans, or a purely British venture.

The Chief Adviser Projects noted the degree of acceptance of compromise that had been secured. Two versions of the aircraft would be required in order to cater for the differing British and German requirements, but there should still be high degree of commonality. In the event that collaboration proved impossible, a purely British venture would involve higher research and development costs of perhaps £100M. In these circumstances the technology of both Rolls-Royce and BAC could be advanced without the frustrations of collaboration. By contrast, a joint undertaking with the French would give BAC less in design and production effort.

For its part, the Defence Secretariat provided a tentative costing of alternative means of fulfilling the attack and reconnaissance roles and of satisfying the later fighter requirement. Collaboration with the French would bring heavy research and development costs, political difficulties and an unequal division of design and production work. The only possible American aircraft ruled itself out on grounds of cost. To attempt to close the gap in attack and reconnaissance capability by increasing orders for existing aircraft, that is to say Jaguar and/or Buccaneer, would impose formidable operational limitations and would be disproportionately expensive in the early years of the ten-year costing period. In the Secretariat's view, therefore, the consortium aircraft was the only option that could satisfy the attack/recce requirement while maintaining expenditure within projected limits.

In closing, I offer these conflicting views to underline some of the risks and uncertainties that were involved in a project to which ministers would shortly have to decide whether or not to commit the UK. There were, of course, a whole range of additional issues related to shared design, research and industrial organisation which had still to be resolved.

EVOLUTION OF THE TORNADO PROJECT
Dr William Stewart

Bill Stewart joined the RAE from Glasgow University in 1942. After a three-year stint with the British Joint Services Mission in Washington he returned to the RAE at its new Thurleigh site in 1956 before moving, via the Imperial Defence College, to the Ministry of Aviation. There he became the project director for the Jaguar, the AFVG and Director General for the MRCA. In 1973 he was appointed Deputy Controller Aircraft which made him Chairman of NAMMO's Board of Directors. By the time that he left MOD(PE) in 1981, he had been involved in the MRCA/Tornado project for some fifteen years. He subsequently worked as a consultant until his final retirement in 1994.

The Tornado evolved at a time of political change, with consequent changes in defence policy, realignments in industry, in relationships between government and industry and the way in which projects were managed within government and industry. In military procurement, a primary feature of the new government policy was collaboration.

In 1965-66, military procurement was in the Ministry of Aviation. The Ministry of Technology had been set up in October 1964 in its original form, primarily concerned with computers, telecommunications and machine tools. It was expanded in 1966 to include other engineering industries and merchant ship building. In 1967, the Ministry of Aviation was merged into the Ministry of Technology. In 1970, aviation was separated out into a Ministry of Aviation Supply and subsequently military procurement was integrated into the Ministry of Defence as the Procurement Executive. Thus, political ministerial responsibility for military procurement was changing in the late '60s; the formative years of Tornado lay within the rapidly expanding Ministry of Technology.

The Plowden Committee, 'set up to consider the future place and organisation of the aircraft industry in the national economy' reported in December 1965, its main conclusions and most of its recommendations being accepted by the government. One of its main recommendations confirmed collaboration with Europe, which had already started earlier in the year with the Anglo-French package of Joint Projects. A further recommendation of the Plowden Committee was that the government should arrange with industry to carry out jointly a full examination into measures to improve efficiency. The joint government-industry Elstub Committee ranged over a number of subjects in the broad fields of project management and selection. The Downey Committee was set up to examine project management arrangements. This resulted in giving Project Directors, who previously held mainly technical responsibilities, total project responsibility, including programme and financial responsibilities. This was applied in the Tornado Project.

The primary objective of the new government's military procurement policy in 1965 was collaboration. The reasons were basically political and economic and covered the following aspects:

a. Political.
b. Industrial.
c. Military.
d. Rationalisation.
e. Standardisation.
f. Interoperability.
g. Advanced technology risk sharing.
h. Large investment required relative to company and government resources.
i. Sharing of development costs.
j. Economy of scale.
k. Wider export markets.

The relative advantages and disadvantages in collaboration depended, of course, on the extent of participation by the countries involved. In the case of Jaguar, the French had a similar industrial capability and technology, an experienced governmental procurement organisation similar to our own and backed by research and development establishments. With equal sharing and aircraft numbers, substantial savings were possible compared to a national project. In the case of other European countries, industrial capacity was much lower than in UK, there was a lack of procurement experience and less R & D support. Thus, in the case of Tornado, substantial disadvantages had to be considered. An assessment was clouded by the way in which the programme evolved. In the early stages, when major decisions were being taken, there were six countries and the emphasis on intended numbers of aircraft left the UK with only a 20% participation. In the eventual production programme, the RAF took almost half of the aircraft. Thus, in retrospect, the UK conceded the build up of a major international industrial/governmental military procurement complex in Munich, contributed a substantially 'greater share of technology' and the backing of our research and development establishments to the project.

It was against this changing background that Tornado evolved from the merging of two distinct lines of activity. First, the UK had been studying variable geometry as a technical solution for a multi-role capability. The French were conducting similar studies. Joint Anglo-French Variable Geometry aircraft studies were set up. Initially, the RAF was seeking a fighter and the French a strike aircraft. Part way through the studies, the UK's defence policy changed the RAF requirement to a strike aircraft, while the French announced that they would convert their Mirage IV to the *Force de Frappe* role and now wanted a fighter. The depth of these studies convinced the UK that variable geometry was a viable solution. When the French withdrew in June 1967, we were able to continue the work at Warton on the development of the swing-wing hinge, new materials and avionics integration. Secondly, Germany, Italy, the Netherlands, Belgium and Canada, who had been operating F-104 aircraft, were discussing together the possibility of jointly developing a replacement, referred to as the NKF, *Neuen Kampfflugzeug*. They had set up a Joint Working Group but kept the UK at arms length until they had prepared some positions and produced their Joint Operational Equipment Objective; only then was the UK included in the discussions. This led to the six countries signing, on 17 July 1968, a Memorandum of Understanding which launched the Conceptual Phase of the MRCA Project.

By the end of 1968, the technical studies were indicating that such an aircraft was feasible; a basis for international industrial participation was emerging and agreements had been achieved for the international management of the project. These negotiations had been conducted by the six nations but at this stage Belgium and Canada left the project. On 14 May 1969, Germany, Italy and the UK agreed to participate in the Project Definition Phase but the Netherlands left the project. A General Memorandum of Understanding set out the principles on which the programme would be conducted and the first of a series of specific MOUs launched the Definition Phase. A wide range of parameters were studied, including alternatives of fixed or variable geometry, single- or two-crew layouts and single- or twin-engined installations. During the Definition Phase, it was recognised that engine development had to start ahead of the intended airframe launch date. The other countries forced a competition between Rolls-Royce, General Electric and Pratt & Whitney. The UK government's support for Rolls-Royce was particularly strong: at that time military and civil engine activities were closely associated within the Ministry of Technology. The UK could not have accepted an American engine in this European Project and such an outcome would have led to the collapse of the programme. With the selection of Rolls-Royce and the formation of Turbo Union, development of the RB 199 was launched in October 1969. Full scale development of the MRCA Project was launched on 20 July 1970.

In addition to the primary objective of providing their forces with a suitable operational aircraft, there are many aspects of an international programme in which the arrangements whereby the aircraft is developed and produced and the programme managed are also of major importance to each of the participating governments. In many cases national objectives conflict and compromises have to be negotiated. In some cases, the collective national objectives do not constitute the most economic conduct of the programme and it is for negotiation to what extent national objectives can be sacrificed in the interests of economy.

In the MRCA programme, some of the important management principles had to be settled immediately. It was decided, that there would be a multi-national governmental organisation and an international industrial organisation with clearly defined weapon responsibility, working in close interrelationship. In creating an international governmental project office, and dealing through it with industry on a contractual basis, involved consideration of the legal framework within which the project should be conducted. Unless the countries are prepared to allow one nation to act for them in placing contracts, which they were not prepared to do, it is necessary to create some international entity.

This was one of the considerations which led the three countries to seek NATO status for the MRCA Project. The NATO Charter for the Multi-Role Combat Aircraft Development and Production Management

Organisation (NAMMO) was granted on 12 August 1969. This established NAMMO as a subsidiary body within the framework of NATO and bestowed upon it the 'juridical personality possessed by NATO', providing it with both a legal status and the authority to conclude contracts and international agreements. Provision was made for the delegation of this authority to a Board of Directors and through them, with certain limitations, to the NAMMA international project office in Munich. All NAMMA staff were to be provided by the three countries and have the grades, staff rules and conditions of NATO personnel.

Early in the governmental negotiations, each of the countries nominated their prime contractors. Various alternative company structures were considered, such as:

a. one of the nominated companies being the prime contractor and sub-contracting to the others;

b. individual companies conducting work, to agreed sharing plans, under contracts let by their own governments, as with Concorde;

c. a 'shell company' whereby all company personnel belonged to their own company and worked within a committee structure, as SEPECAT did for Jaguar; or

d. an independent joint international company with its own staff and premises, separate from the parent companies.

In the event it was the last option that was adopted and Panavia was duly set up in Munich.. It had originally been anticipated that Panavia would have overall responsibility for the complete system but, following the selection of the RB 199 engine, it was later decided that the government organisation would handle engine development directly with a separate joint company, Turbo Union. Another exception to the rule concerned the gun, in that the governments placed the contract direct with Mauser.

While the UK, with its large industrial capability and the support of the government research establishments at Farnborough, Pyestock and Malvern could dominate the technical solution, the UK had much less political voice in the more general arrangements for the programme. Many major decisions were taken in the early stage of the programme when six countries had been involved. Early on, it was decided in principle that the sharing of work and cost would be in proportion to the

Date	UK	FRG	Italy	Others	Total
1968	300	550	200	600	1500
	20%	36.7%	13.3%	30%	100%
1969	385	600	200	100	1285
	30%	46.7%	15.5%	7.8%	100%
1970	385	420	100	-	905
	42.5%	46.5%	11%	-	100%
1972	385	324	100	-	809
	47.6%	40%	12.4%	-	100%

Fig 1. Progressive Changes in the Weighting of National Commitments to the MRCA Project, 1968-72.

number of aircraft purchased and in these early stages had to be based on declared numbers. It was hoped that other considerations would be taken into account but these tended to be contentious or conflicting and work sharing was virtually dictated by aircraft numbers. The numbers declared are tabulated in Fig 1:

In 1968, the declared numbers were: UK 300; Germany 550; Italy 200 and the other three countries 600 for a total of 1500 aircraft. Thus, in the Conceptual Phase, when many decisions in relation to the conduct of the programme had to be taken, the UK's share was only 20%. This was due to: the involvement of *six* countries; *under*statement by the UK, until the Air Defence Variant was introduced and *over*statement by Germany. When the UK increased its numbers to 385 in 1969 Germany simply raised its bid to 600 and with the departure of Belgium and Canada, the UK's share was still only 30%. With the start of the Full Development phase in 1970, the German numbers fell from 600 to 420 and at the start of production in 1972 this fell further to 324.

The general principles of work sharing agreed by the governments were:

    a. The objective is maximum cost effectiveness compatible with work sharing formulae in designated areas.

b. Each defined area is to be self-contained.
   c. The quality of technology is to be balanced.
   d. Airframe and engine companies to be nominated by governments.
   e. All airframe equipment, engine accessories and avionic items to be selected by competitive tender.
   f. Encouragement is to be given to collaborative proposals.
   g. Selection procedures were to be laid down by governments.

For airframe and engine work sharing, specific governmental directives were:

   a. Cost effective distribution between nominated companies to defined formulae.
   b. Balance of quality of technology.
   c. System design responsibility principle for individual design or sub-system areas.
   d. Clear allocation of responsibilities.
   e. No duplication of work.

Equipment selection inevitably presents problems with conflicting interests and competition between countries and within countries. While the procedures for selecting equipment must involve the prime contractor deeply, important items are very much associated with national industrial policy and can only be resolved by the governments concerned. Thus the equipments for Tornado were divided into four categories:

   A. Supply by governments. Company only concerned with integration into aircraft.
   B. Selection by governments. Company involved in specifications, requests for proposals and evaluation.
   C. Selection by company, but government approval of required.
   D. Selection by company, governments only to be informed.

About 40% of equipment was selected by governments (Category B) and some 60% by the company (Category C). None of the Category C items were vetoed by the governments.

In summary, although the Royal Air Force took the largest number of production aircraft, the UK was handicapped in some of the major decisions taken early in the programme because the declared numbers gave the UK only a 20% voice. As a result, the UK had to accept that the industrial/government complex would be established in Munich.

Nevertheless, there was a determination to make this arrangement work and the substantial contributions made by the UK's industry, its government officials and its research establishments ensured the project's success. The UK's permanent Chairman of NAMMO's Board of Directors maintained continuity in the overall direction of the programme and British industrial leadership within the technical and contractual divisions of NAMMA ensured an excellent operational aircraft at well contained costs. Although there were attempts in various areas to introduce American influence into the project, with the exception of the radar (developed in the USA but 'productionised' in Europe), the programme was entirely European and established a basis for European military procurement collaboration.

TORNADO/MRCA - ESTABLISHING COLLABORATIVE PARTNERSHIPS and AIRFRAME TECHNOLOGY
Gerrie Willox

Gerrie Willox joined Bristols from Cranfield University in 1954 before moving to Handley Page and then English Electric. At Warton he worked on the AFVG and UKVG projects until 1967. He subsequently played a leading role in the definition of the MRCA and stayed with the project in various capacities, including wearing a Panavia hat, while his parent company evolved via BAC into British Aerospace for whom he acted as Tornado Project Director and subsequently Director of Projects for the Warton Division. In 1986 he was appointed Managing Director of Eurofighter GmbH in Munich where he remained until his retirement in 1991. Since then he has been a consultant to the aerospace industry.

Introduction

BAC had virtually no say in its choice of partners when, in 1968, the UK Government joined an existing collaborative programme in which the other nations had already nominated their representative companies. Even if there had been a free choice, however, BAC would almost certainly have opted for the companies that were already involved, MBB, Fiat and Fokker, although the latter withdrew shortly after the formation of the central management company.

BAC's Warton Division had been working on variable sweep projects, complemented by back-up aerodynamic and structural test programmes, since 1963 so they were able to contribute five year's experience and a substantial technology database to the early MRCA/Tornado project. MBB was the only other company with any experience of variable sweep, having previously worked on some joint projects with the Americans.

Initial feasibility studies done in 1968 were carried out independently with little exchange of technical data, the results of these studies being submitted to the sponsor governments in January 1969. They showed that an MRCA was feasible but that considerable differences would have to be resolved in order to arrive at a common configuration.

Joint industrial studies were begun with a view to solving this problem, a degree of urgency being injected by governmental advice to the effect that a solution was required by the end of March to avoid jeopardising the entire programme. Such was the spirit of co-operation that, without compromising the validity of the technology, a joint configuration had been agreed by the end of February. In terms of the airframe, the major differences were that the German Air Force had wanted a single-engined single-seater, whilst the RAF had wanted a twin-engined two-seater. Based on the findings of cost-effectiveness studies carried out by BAC on the single- *versus* twin-engined options, Germany had quickly agreed to accept a twin-engined design. On the other hand, it took more than a year to persuade the Germans that the cockpit workload on the MRCA would be such as to require two men to ensure maximum effectiveness of the weapon system. As a result, in March 1970 all participants accepted that the design of the IDS would be based on two seats and two engines. There were, however, national variations in avionic and weapons fits.

To give the project the best possible chance of success, and to ensure the most efficient utilisation of each company's skills and manpower, system design responsibilities and workshare were agreed early on as was the constitution of the joint engineering management committee structure.

Establishing Collaborative Partnerships
When the UK joined the project, which was then called MRA75, the consortium consisted of Germany, Italy, Belgium, Holland and Canada; at that point the project was renamed MRCA. Until the end of 1968, project studies were carried out independently, Belgium and Canada withdrawing during that first year. Since the remaining industrial participants had already been nominated, BAC's partners were:

Germany	MBB
Italy	Fiat
Holland	Fokker

Virtually all of the project design studies and parametric work in the early days was carried out by BAC and MBB; Fiat and Fokker being involved only to a very minor degree.

Airframe Technology
At Warton, serious project work on variable geometry had begun with the P45 trainer/light fighter in 1963. Even before this, however, a considerable amount of work had already been carried out at the

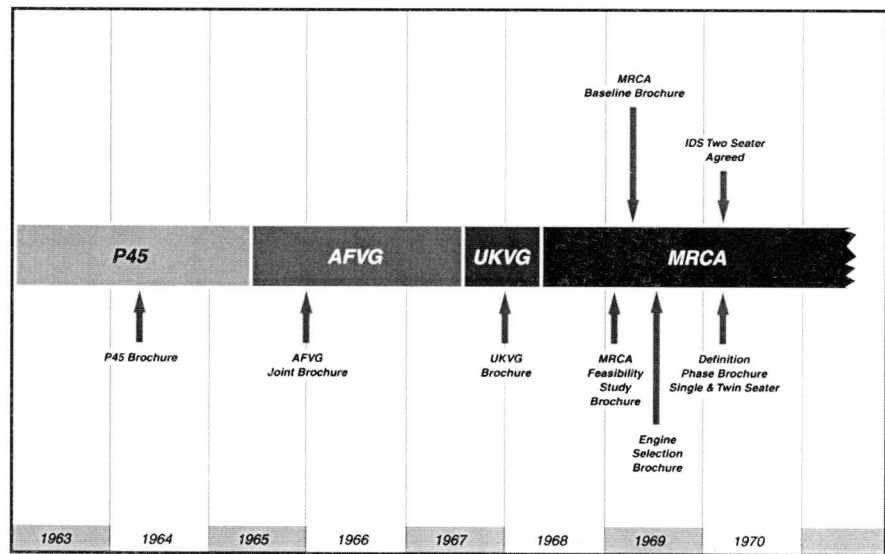

Fig 1. History of VG Project Studies at Warton.

Weybridge Division which had demonstrated, experimentally, the feasibility of rotating the complete wing under load. Major problems which still remained to be solved included the identification of a satisfactory bearing material for the pivot assembly and the selection of a material suitable for the wing/fuselage seal. There were also many aerodynamic problems associated with the advanced configuration.

The history of variable geometry studies, which included back-up experimental work, at BAC's Warton Division is shown in Figure 1 and the continuity of design experience is illustrated at Figure 2. Throughout this period, BAC carried out many wind tunnel tests on models at both subsonic and supersonic speeds. The aerodynamicists were very keen on a fuselage-mounted pivot which permitted the provision of a full-span leading edge high lift device with the wing in the forward sweep position, although it also resulted in a considerable shift in the aerodynamic centre when the wing was swept. Meanwhile, considerable experimental work on the pivot, its bearing and the surrounding structure was being carried out on an appropriate rig which eventually pointed to the selection of Teflon for the pivot bearing. Another purpose-built rig enabled the

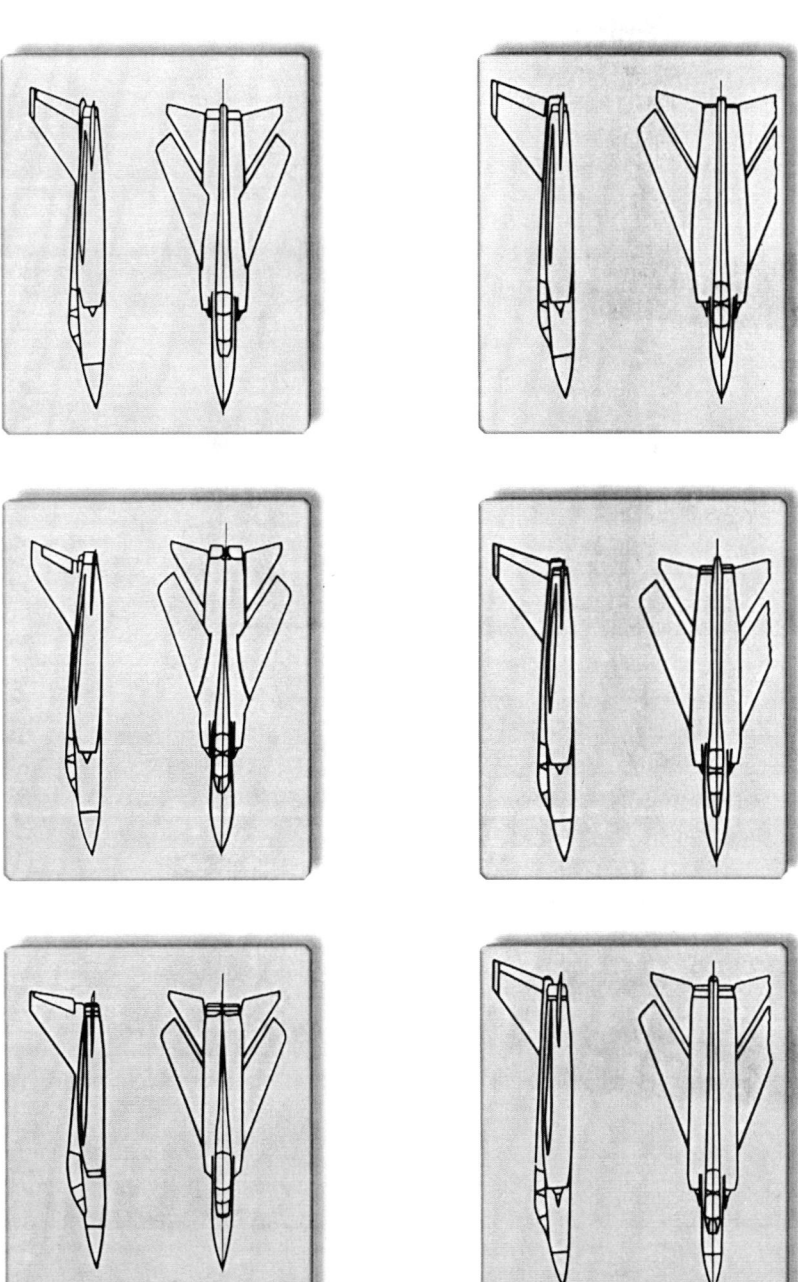

Fig 2. Continuity of VG Design within BAC.

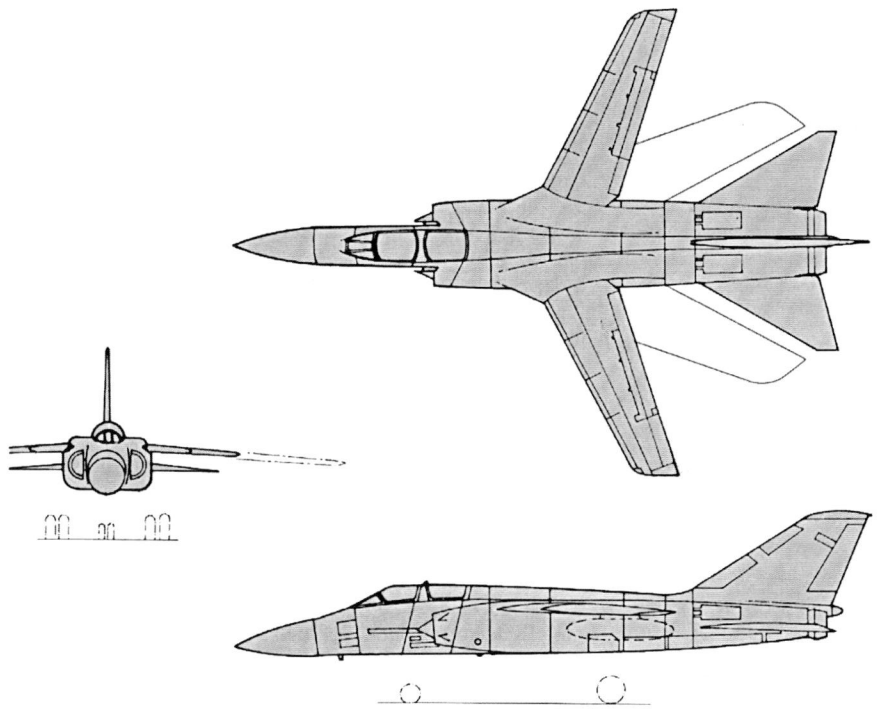

Fig 3. General Arrangement of AFVG.

designers to develop an inflatable wing seal made from a rubber compound developed by a local company.

Project work on the P45 eventually ceased in 1965, when agreement was reached with the French on both the Jaguar and AFVG programmes. Within a few months of BAC's starting work on the AFVG, a joint brochure was issued in collaboration with Dassault showing the configuration at Figure 3.

Agreement had been reached on most aspects of the design, one notable exception being the location of the position of the pivot pin. BAC favoured a pin mounted just inboard of the fuselage side with a retractable nib; Dassault wanted it just outboard of the fuselage side with a fixed nib. The engine installation was another key design feature on which agreement had not been reached, BAC advocating a drop-out arrangement whilst Dassault preferred inserting the engine from the rear.

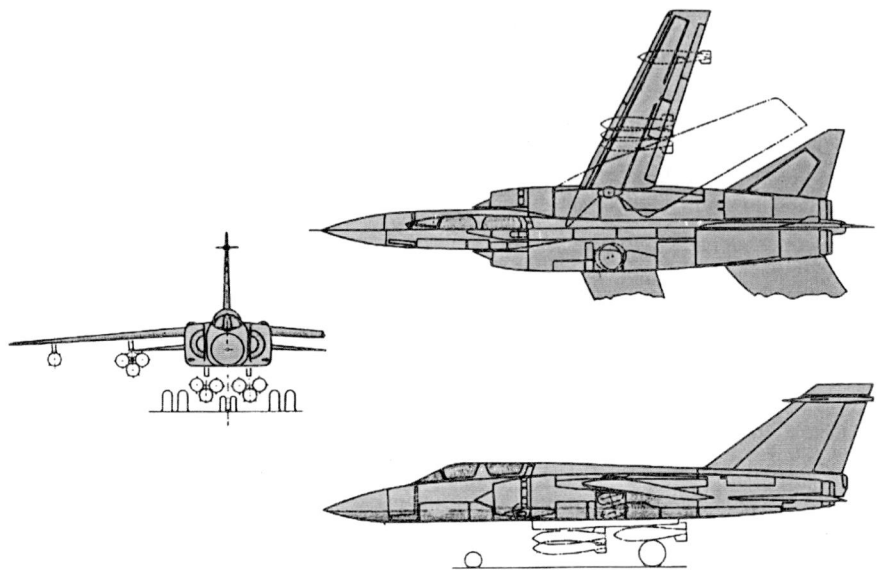

Fig 4. General Arrangement of UKVG

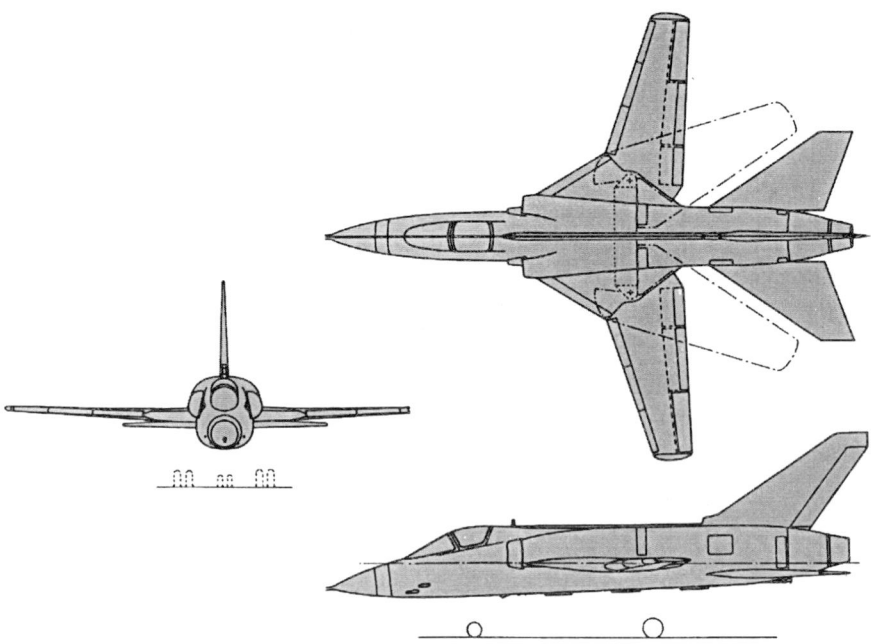

Fig 5. General Arrangement of NKF.

A joint engineering study was to have been undertaken to resolve these issues but this was never carried out due to Dassault's increasing concentration on the Mirage G. Note, incidentally, that the intake, would have been a semi-conical arrangement similar to those of the of the Mirage series and the TSR2.

When the French withdrew BAC continued to work on the project alone, the final configuration of the UKVG being shown at Figure 4. This layout, with its fuselage-mounted pin, retractable nib and drop-out engine installation, more or less represented BAC's lead-in to the MRCA feasibility studies of 1968.

On the German side, MBB had begun VG project work on the AVS (Advanced Vertical Strike) in conjunction with Fairchild Republic. This was an extremely complex VG-V/STOL project which was soon cancelled on cost grounds. This led MBB to commence work on the NKF (*Neuen Kampflugzeug*) in 1967 to meet a German Air Force requirement for a strike fighter (Figure 5). This design, which featured a single engine,

***Fig 6**. MRCA - Required Characteristics.*

shoulder intakes and an outboard pin with a large fixed nib, represented MBB's baseline when initial MRCA studies began in 1968.

As Figure 6 makes clear, the MRCA's very varied mission requirements gave rise to conflicting design parameters which, using the technology available at the time, could be reconciled only by an aircraft having variable sweep and an afterburning fan engine employing a thrust reverser.

On completion of initial independent feasibility studies, brochures were submitted in January 1969. The proposals submitted by BAC and MBB are illustrated at Figures 7 and 8 respectively. As I have already indicated, the major problem was that the British wanted their twin-engined two-seater whilst the Germans were after a single-engined single-seater.

When the engineering teams got together in February 1969, therefore, they had to answer the following questions, and, if the project were to survive, quickly:
- One or two engines?
- Type of Engine Installation?
- Wing and Tailplane position on Fuselage?
- Pin Position?
- Fixed or Retractable Nib?
- Intake Type?
- Single- or Two-Seat?
- Fuel in Wing?
- Type of Flight Control System?
- Wing Centre Box Material?
- Hydraulic Pressure and Pipe Material?

As regards the number of engines, BAC had carried out a relevant MOD(UK)-funded study in 1967/68. This had shown that the twin-engined option was more cost-effective, largely due to its ability to cope with an engine failure. This study was persuasive enough to persuade MBB to agree that the baseline configuration should have two engines.

As previously noted, MBB wanted the engine installed from the rear whilst BAC's engineers were convinced that the only way to meet the specified engine change time was to have a drop-out installation. After much investigation of the implication of these options, particularly on the rear fuselage structure and the tailplane frame, and anticipating that BAC

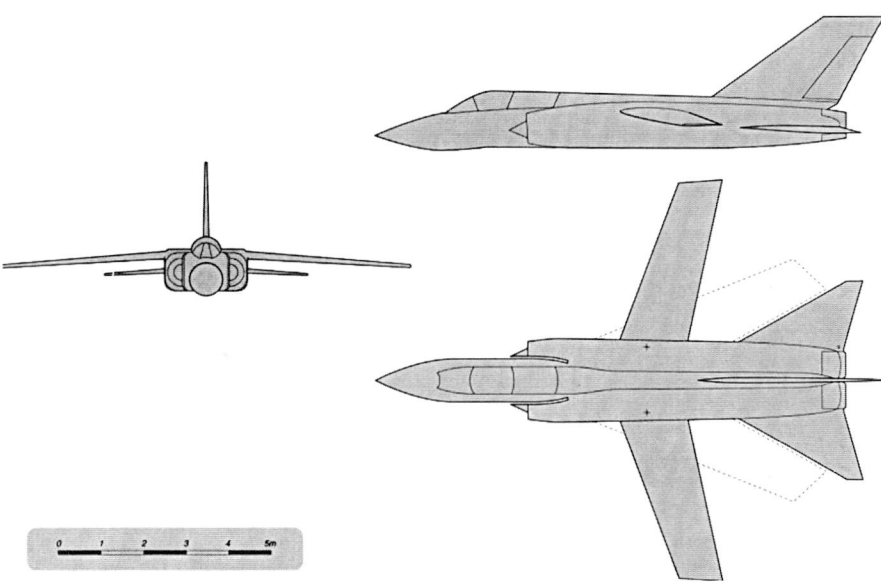

Fig 7. BAC Two-Seat Feasibility Study

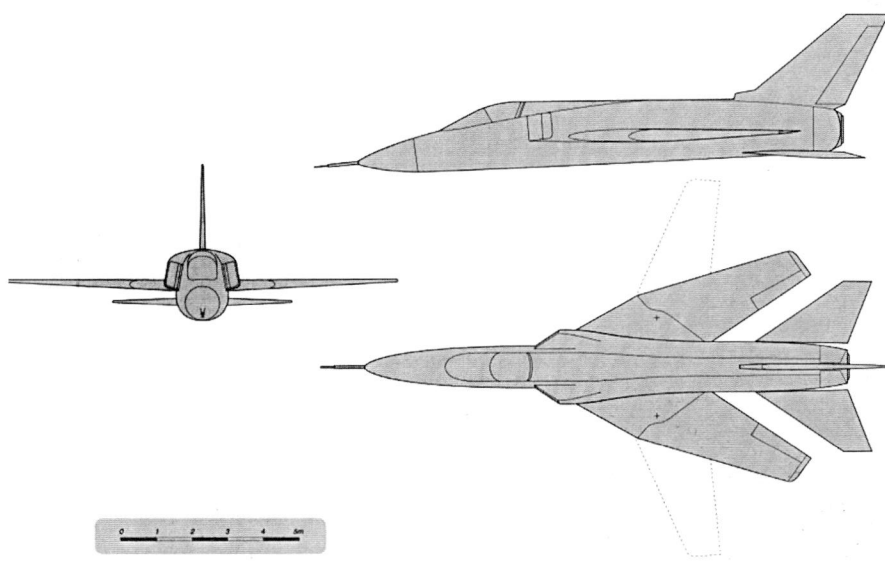

Fig 8. MBB Single-Seat Feasibility Study

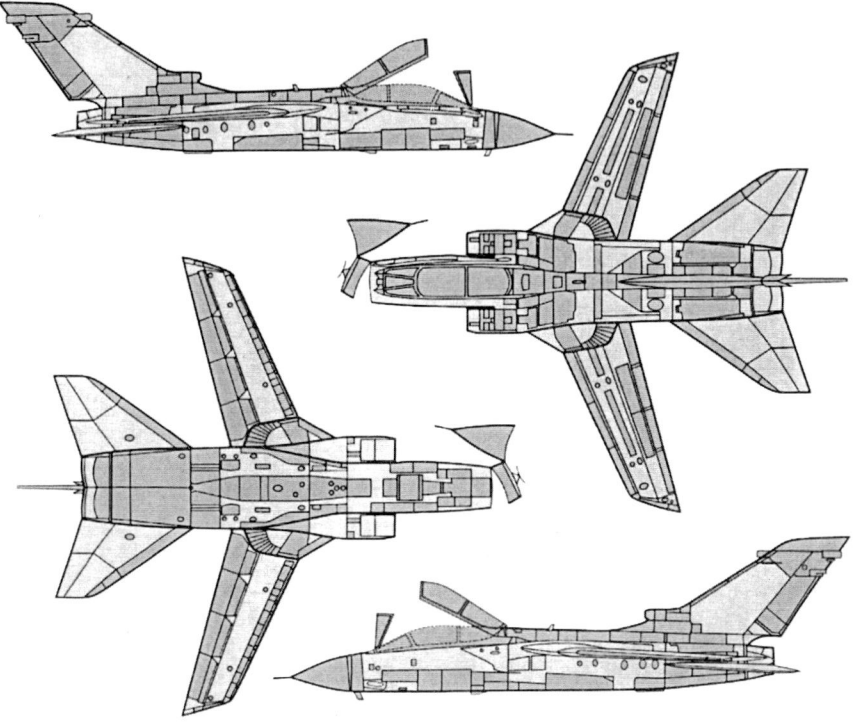

Fig 9. *Location of access panels.*

were likely to have responsibility for the rear fuselage, the drop-out solution was eventually adopted. It is pertinent to remark here that, at this early stage, easy access to the aircraft systems was recognised as being essential in order to meet the demanding maintenance requirements and the locations of most of the access panels (as shown in Figure 9) were agreed at this stage.

The aerodynamicists were able to agree that the tailplane should be positioned below the plane of the wing in order to ensure acceptable lift/pitch characteristics and, having agreed the drop-out engine installation, this allowed for a high wing with a mid-position tailplane. MBB had favoured a mid-wing with a low tailplane which, in BAC's opinion, would have given rise to structural problems.

After much engineering debate, both as regards structure and aerodynamics, a pin position just outboard of the fuselage side was agreed. The further outboard the pin is positioned, the less the aerodynamic centre shifts when the wing is swept. Taking this into account, the pivot is actually located at 23% of the wing span measured from the centreline of the aircraft.

Because the leading edge sweep of the nib affects the formation of the upper surface vortices (the higher the sweep the stronger the vortices) a 60° swept nib with the wing in the fully swept position was agreed. At this stage, however, BAC was not prepared to accept a fixed nib because of possible adverse affects on lift with the wing in the forward sweep position, so the configuration as initially submitted had a retractable nib, which allowed for the provision of full span leading edge devices. A few months later, however, in March 1970, after carrying out a great deal of low speed wind tunnel testing to optimise the camber of the nib to ensure stable vortices beyond the stall, BAC agreed to a fixed nib.

As regards the intakes, an entirely new shape was devised based upon the need for good performance recovery at high incidence at M1·8. All available data indicated that, under these conditions, a horizontal wedge was superior to both vertical wedge and conical type intakes. Note that the intake is positioned well forward of the wing, allowing for a good settling length for the airflow to the engine and thus good pressure distribution at the engine face.

As regards single-seat versus two-seat, BAC was initially unable to persuade MBB that the workload for only one crew member would be excessive in an MRCA type aircraft so both twin- and single-seat variants were submitted; Figure 10 represents the baseline single-seat configuration. Over the next year, however, BAC was able to use the crew workload mock-up to demonstrate, to the satisfaction of both MBB and the German Air Force, that a two-man crew was essential if the weapon system was to be operated to maximum effect.

When submitting twin and single seaters in March 1969, it was agreed that, to contain costs, changes to the airframe should be minimal so the same fuselage length was maintained for both variants, as shown in Figure 11. The second seat occupied a space that had previously been a fuel tank in MBB's single-seater. MBB had originally opposed using the wings as integral fuel tanks but, needing to compensate for the fuel displaced by the second crew member, and reassured by BAC's experience with integral fuel tanks in the wings of the Lightning, TSR2

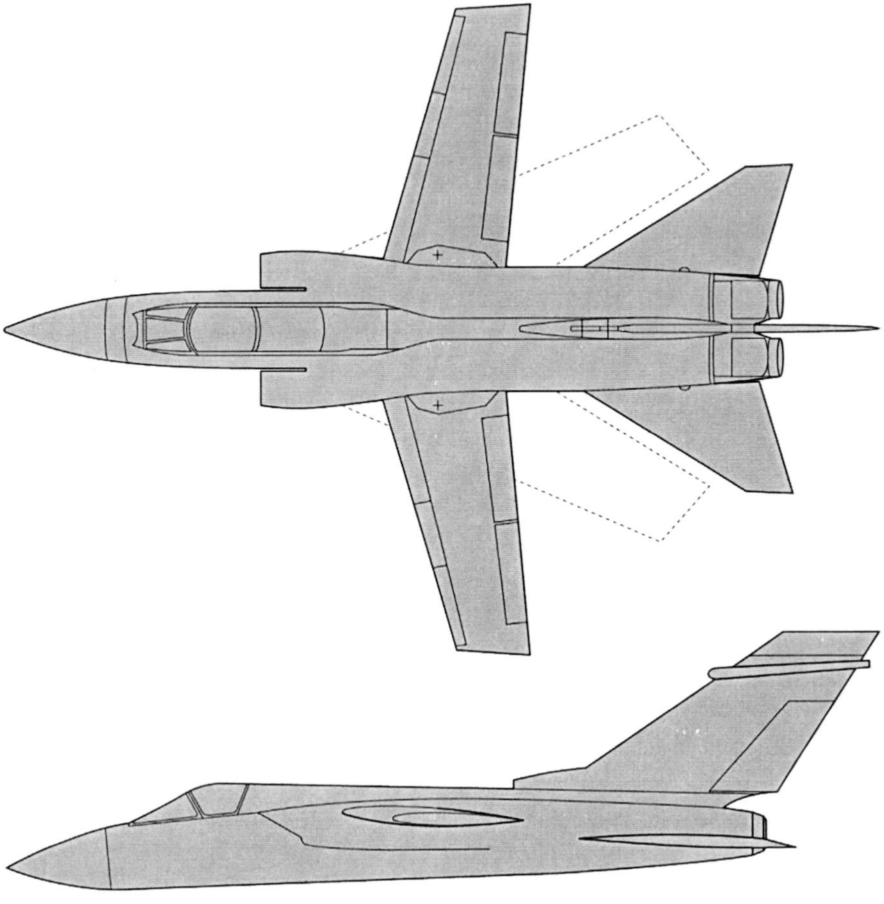

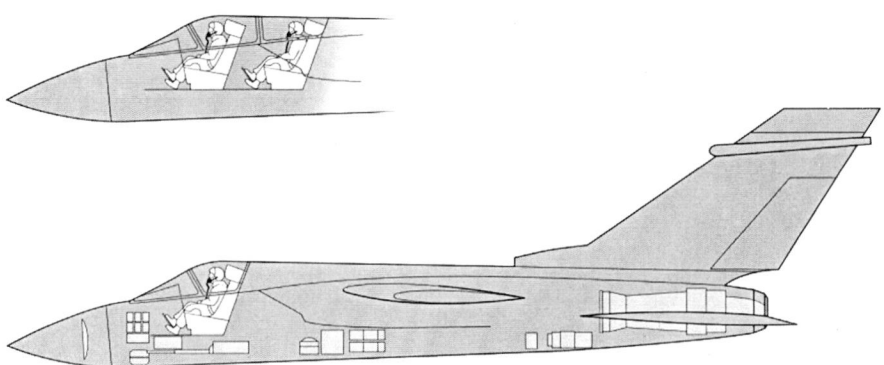

Figs 10 & 11. *Baseline Configuration and Two-Seat Option.*

and Jaguar, MBB had accepted this solution by March 1970 when the two-seat IDS variant was finalised. Fiat, incidentally, had never had any problem agreeing to integral wing tanks.

When the engineering teams first got together in February 1969, BAC's proposal for the pilot's cockpit was based on the work it had already done on the UKVG project. While this provided a baseline it was extensively revised in the course of many meetings of the cockpit committee. While both cockpits featured head-up and moving map displays, the Tornado cockpit is far more advanced than the original concept and has many more electronic displays. In this case, design-by-committee seems to have been a success, since pilots apparently appreciate both the layout of the cockpit and its roominess.

Moving on to the flight control system, MBB were advocating the solution which was finally adopted while BAC were proposing a less technically advanced approach. The solution that was selected was an analogue triplex system (fly-by-wire) with mechanical back-up only to the tailplane. The triplex system depends on comparing signals from two of the lanes; when there is a double failure the rudder centralises and there is only back up on roll and pitch from the tailerons. When this system was adopted it was appreciated that it would involve a great deal of development work but time has shown that it was the correct solution and the excellent flying characteristics of the aircraft are due in no small measure to the flight control system with its computerised flight controller (the Command and Stability Augmentation System - CSAS) which provides automatic control and damping of angular motion and compensates for configuration changes during flight by sensing accelerations about all three axes. The CSAS compares these movements with those demanded by the pilot and automatically corrects any difference. In addition, the system uses data on altitude, speed and aerodynamic configuration to optimise control responses.

One of the biggest problems facing the engineers was meeting the empty mass target for the aircraft and, as a result, advanced materials were utilised wherever feasible. The breakdown of the structural material content for the airframe in terms of mass is:

Light Alloy	71%
Titanium	18%
Steel	6%
Other	5%

The major titanium item is the wing centre box which is of all-welded construction. Since MBB lacked the necessary equipment, manufacture of this component was initially subcontracted to Grumman in the USA. To further minimise mass it was agreed that the aircraft should have a 4000 psi hydraulic system using titanium pipes. Based on results obtained from the rig at BAC, Teflon was selected for the pin bearing material. The design of the wing/fuselage seal was also based on data obtained from BAC's rig testing programme.

After a year of definition phase work a comprehensive brochure, covering all design aspects, was submitted in March 1970. Single- and two-seat versions were still being promoted at this stage but all of the participants soon agreed to adopt the two-seat IDS and the configuration at that time is shown in Figure 12.

By this time the layout closely resembled the eventual Tornado as shown at Figure 13. The main external differences are confined to such subtleties as the shape of the wing tips, the location of the environmental control system's air intake at the base of the fin and the design of the trailing edge fin/fuselage junction. It is perhaps worth stressing that, because the Tornado was intended to carry a variety of external stores of widely differing sizes, a great deal of attention had had to be paid to the contouring of the fuselage underside and to the retraction path of the undercarriage.

The division of workshare and technical responsibility was agreed early on, the outcome being illustrated at Figure 14. In essence, responsibility for general equipment and common avionic components was related to its location within the airframe, whilst nationally specified avionic equipment was the responsibility of the respective national companies.

The allocation of responsibility for system design is shown in Figure 15. Each company could, of course, study any technical aspects affecting the overall design if they so wished. It was the usual practice, however, for one company to have overall responsibility for a specific technical aspect with the others carrying out checks as appropriate.

Finally, Figure 16 shows the major engineering management structure. This management system worked very well, due to an early willingness to reach agreement: an approach which, on the whole, continued throughout the programme. Detailed aspects were solved by

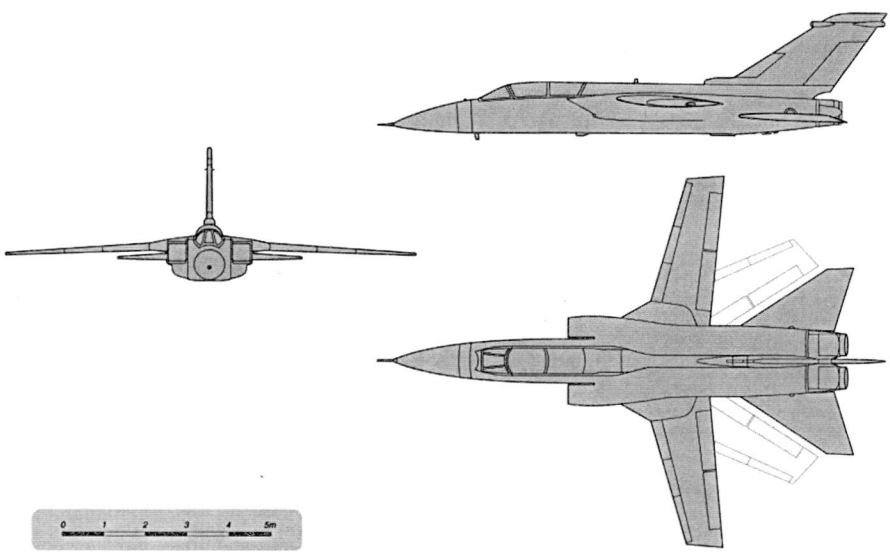

Fig 12. Definition Phase – Final Configuration.

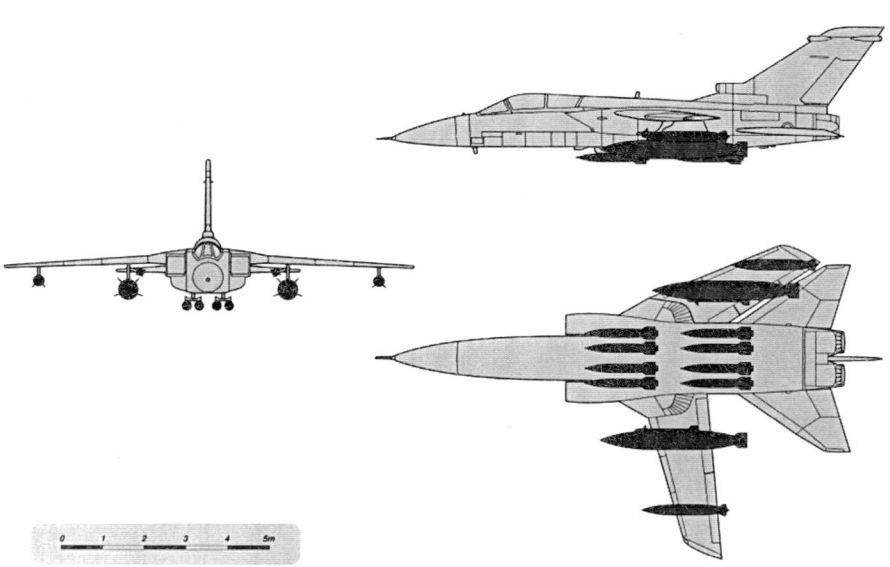

Fig 13. Tornado IDS.

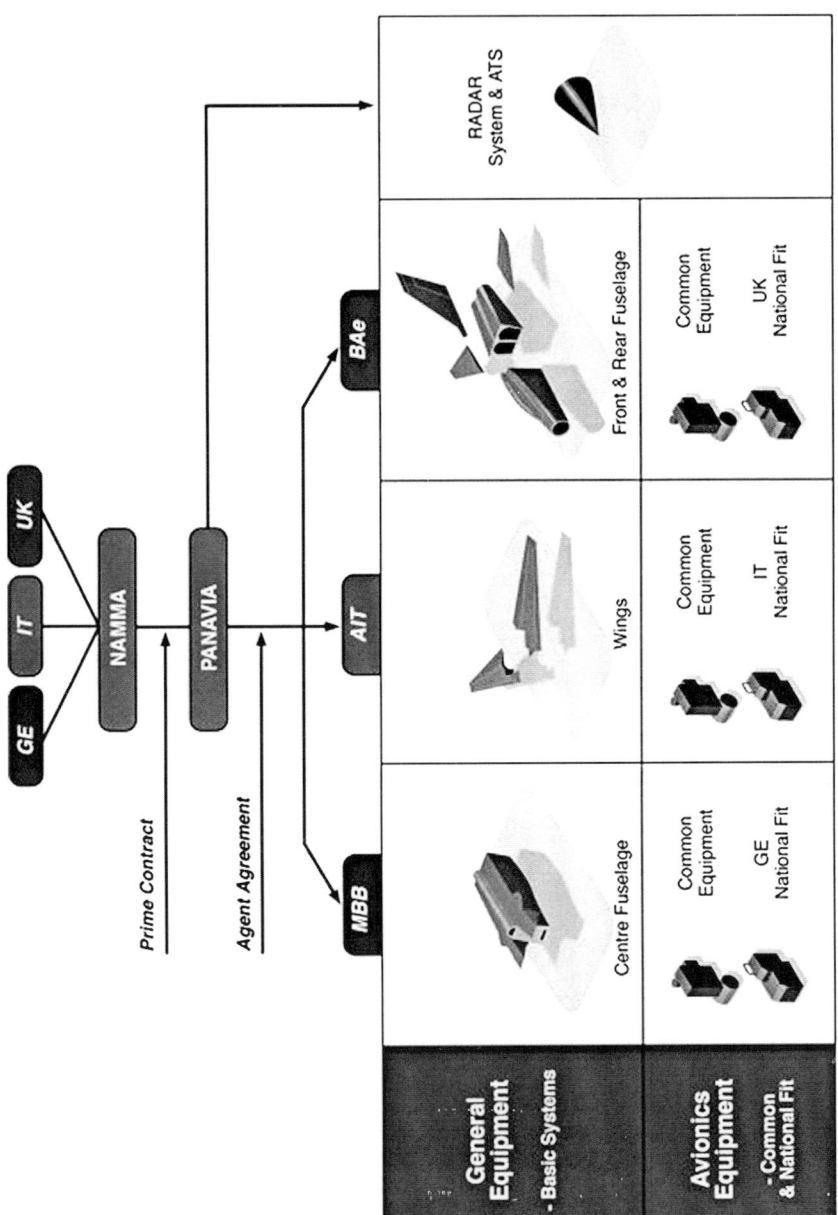

Fig 14. Division of Workshare and Technical Responsibility.

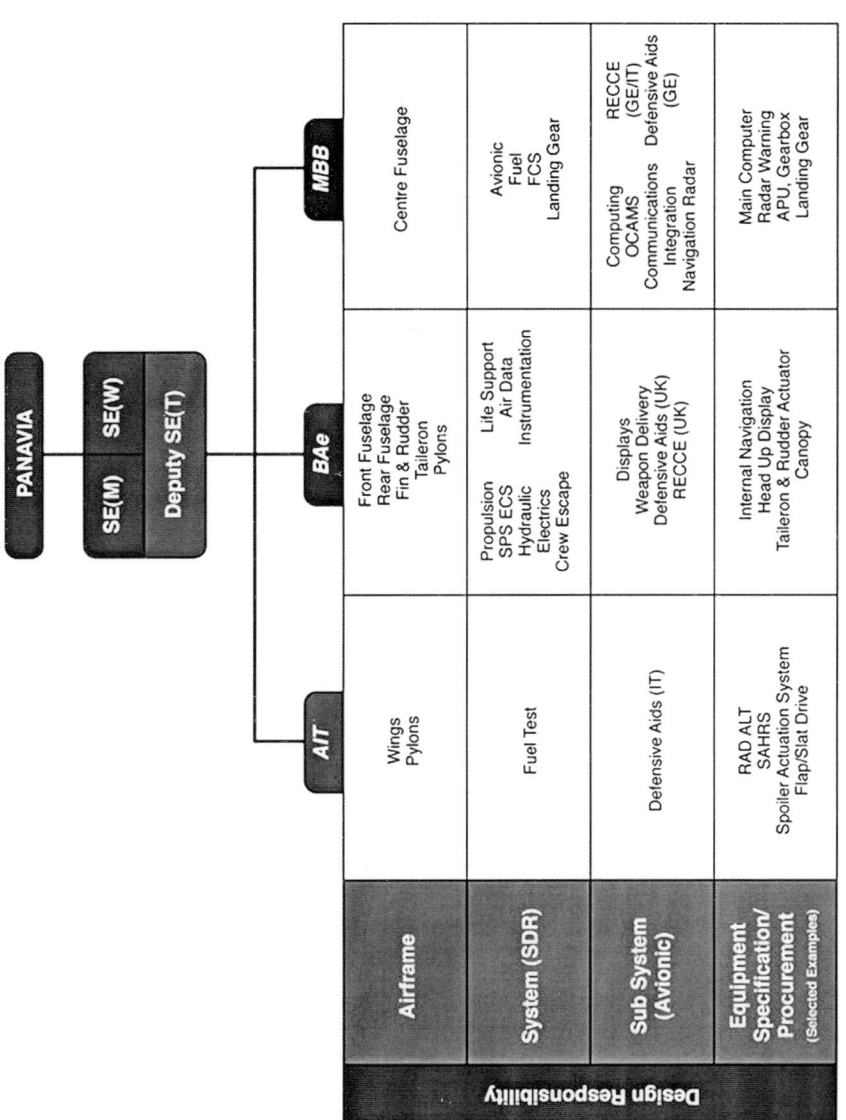

Fig 15. Systems Design Responsibility.

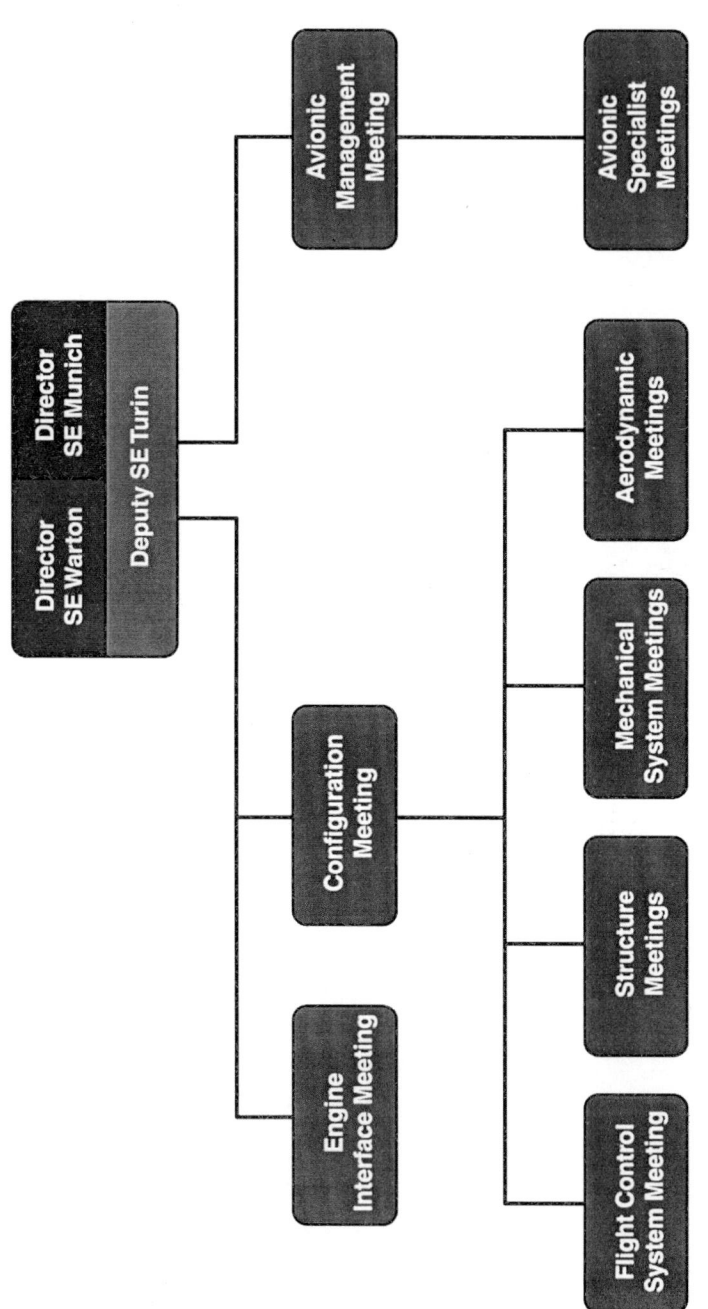

Fig 16. Engineering Management Tree.

direct negotiation between appropriate specialists, but to manage a weapon system of this complexity it was also necessary to hold formal monthly top-level meetings to resolve any major problems. There were differences at times but I found that in the end common engineering sense usually prevailed with the solution that was felt to be in the best interests of the project being selected.

Acknowledgement
The author would like to thank BAE SYSTEMS and their local Heritage Society at Warton for allowing access to the necessary documents and to BAE SYSTEMS for allowing the report to be produced on their facilities; however, the views expressed are those of the author.

RB 199 – THE ENGINE FOR TORNADO
Dr Gordon Lewis

Gordon Lewis joined Bristols from Oxford University in 1944 and from then until his retirement, from the post of Technical Director, Rolls-Royce, in 1986, he was continuously involved in the design and development of all Bristol-based gas turbines. His innovative thinking led to the concept for the vectored thrust Pegasus engine for which he gained several international awards. He was Chief Engineer for the proposed engine for the AFVG and subsequently the MRCA which led to his appointment as Managing Director of Turbo Union for the Tornado programme. In 1983 he was responsible for the initiation of a technology demonstrator programmes in preparation for the EJ200 engine for the Eurofighter/Typhoon.

Summary

It was essential that Rolls-Royce should play a leading role in the next advanced military engine, accepting that it would be the subject of European collaboration. It was also clear that the preservation of an indigenous military engine capability was in the national interest and in the long term interest of the whole UK aerospace industry.

It was, therefore, not advantageous to the MRCA programme that a competitive framework had to be set up with the US engine companies being encouraged to offer ambitious specifications. This was to the detriment of transparent co-operative studies and contributed to the absence of a structured rig and engine demonstrator programme to precede full launch.

In response to the formal Request for Proposal Rolls-Royce decided to offer a fully collaborative programme with comprehensive technology transfer to the German and Italian companies, a commitment expected to be attractive to those countries and unlikely to be offered by the US. Together with a detailed and competitive technical proposal this resulted in the selection of the RB 199 in September 1969.

Joint Company arrangements had been put in place for the competitive phase and these were successfully retained throughout the programme. Responsibilities were rapidly defined and plans made for worksharing of the basic engine and the many accessory items that made up the complete power plant.

The technology reach was necessarily significant in the absence of pre-launch demonstration and problems were evident as soon as the first engine went to test in September 1971. The initial attempts to solve these were frustrated by serious industrial problems in the UK and not helped by the entry into receivership of Rolls-Royce. The enterprise survived a crisis of confidence as engine deficiencies persisted and the flight test programme suffered some delays.

In overcoming the inherent problems affecting the programme the collaborating teams demonstrated their ability to be mutually supportive and objective in decision taking. The experience gained was valuable for the next European project, Typhoon, not least in the implementation of an effective demonstrator phase to synchronise the engine and airframe programmes.

The Requirement

The Tornado required significant advances in thrust-to-weight ratio, in fuel consumption and dictated compact dimensions such that no existing engine could achieve the set objectives. The incorporation of a thrust reverser was an additional feature not common to previous fighter engines.

The specification issued by Panavia necessitated the design of a new engine to operate at high turbine temperature and pressure ratios with a relatively high by-pass ratio to achieve the low fuel consumption sought for the low level mission. The mechanical design had to make use of advanced manufacturing techniques and materials.

Background

There were two major engine companies in the UK when TSR 2 was cancelled in 1965: Rolls-Royce, who were evolving the RB 211 and collaborating with Germany on engines for VTOL aircraft, and Bristol Siddeley, who were committed to engines for Concorde and Harrier and collaborating with France on a family of engines for Anglo-French military projects.

The AFVG was cancelled by France and the German VTOL projects were progressively abandoned. Thus two main streams of advanced engine studies were current when Rolls-Royce acquired Bristol Siddeley in 1966. These were characterised by the two-spool arrangement at Bristol and Derby's three spools.

While two-spool work was by then being conducted on a UK-only basis the three-spool approach was to be the subject of an advanced component programme in collaboration with Germany.

When the MRCA surfaced in 1968 both engine projects were applicable and competing for company support. It was essential for a choice to be made to shape up against the emerging US competition. While the case for the two-spool engine, by then based on the Pegasus configuration, was very strong for the military application the three-spool formula was being vigorously promoted with considerable future potential in the civil market. The German company and officials supported the RB 199 concept and the plan for a joint advanced engineering programme.

Competition

In 1968 Rolls-Royce took the decision to promote the RB 199 and for the programme to be the responsibility of the Bristol Division. The Bristol team had, therefore, to adapt to a design transferred from the other house and to new collaborative partners. This process coincided with a period of intense activity to respond to the airframe requirements for engine data to suit either a single or a twin-engine aircraft and to the Government agencies involved.

As the participating countries reduced to the UK, Germany and Italy, Fiat was brought into the consortium alongside Rolls-Royce and *Motoren und Turbinen-Union* (MTU). It was decided to offer a fully collaborative programme and the appropriate Joint Company arrangements were put in place.

It was apparent that among the German officials and Air Force there was a preference for an American engine, partly for reasons extraneous to the MRCA programme. The RB 199 was viewed with concern by British Aerospace who doubted that a completely new design could be brought to an adequate standard in time for the flight test programme. No developed engine of appropriate size existed to power the first prototype.

While the airframe suppliers had been selected and were able to proceed with a definitive design, the engine companies were called upon to enter a competitive bid against Pratt and Whitney and General Electric. Sixty days was allocated for a comprehensive response to the Request for Proposal.

It was made clear that, to succeed, the RB 199 proposal had to be competitive with the US offerings, with sufficient supporting design and test data to confer credibility on the timescale for development. The fully collaborative plan was included in the response, with technology transfer to MTU and Fiat, and a commitment to an incentive and penalty form of contract. The extensive proposal documentation was delivered to the Agency in Munich on time, and in September 1969 the selection of the RB 199 was announced.

Organisation

Turbo-Union Ltd. (TU) was registered in the UK to negotiate contracts, to allocate work to the partner companies and to account for revenue and expenditure. A small office was set up in Munich for liaison with Panavia and NAMMA, while all aspects of the programme were co-ordinated by Working Groups formed from staff in the participating companies, reporting to the Turbo-Union Management Meeting.

Reliance was placed on communication, in particular using corporate jet aircraft for movement of components and personnel, avoiding the need for a large TU administration. This light organisation, set up initially to process the response to the RFP, was retained through the development programme. Advantages were economy, evolution of understanding between teams, direct decision taking by responsible parties in each company and flexibility as the content of the programme evolved.

Contract

Turbo-Union's commercial proposals were not accepted in their entirety by NAMMA; in particular extensive monitoring and sanctioning procedures were required, together with changes to the proposed TU guarantees. These could not be accepted by TU without variation of the financial terms, and after protracted negotiations the programme proceeded on traditional lines with an Engine Management Group set up by NAMMA.

Design and Development

Full launch was not preceded by demonstration or definitive rig testing. Advanced designs with new features and new manufacturing processes were necessary. A priority decision was taken to eliminate as many high risk mechanical features in the original concept design as possible, to ensure a high level of mechanical integrity and structural safety. This was achieved, although at the expense of a small weight penalty.

The first complete engine test took place in September 1971 and development commenced to address a performance deficit against the very ambitious specification. As the programme advanced other problems surfaced, notably HP turbine blade failures, oil and air system deficiencies, and engine control and handling problems. The latter were severely aggravated by the Tornado's air intakes which presented the engine with a high level of inlet air flow distortion.

Of particular note, with difficult business and political consequences, was the failure of a major contractor to provide the electronic engine control units. The programme had to be restored by exceptional effort at Rolls-Royce to design and manufacture suitable units in-house.

Through the development and flight test period parts supply problems were acute with the need for rapid changes to build standards. This was very severely affected by industrial disputes in the UK. Initial Flight Clearance was delayed by some months and the first Tornado flight eventually took place in August 1974 with derated engines. Engine supply thereafter was critical and the flight test programme was slowed down by the substandard nature of the early engines.

Some problems persisted into initial service operation, the low life of early HP turbine blades presenting the Services with parts supply and engine overhaul difficulties. These shortfalls necessitated the clearance of a succession of improved engine standards and the upgrading of delivered engines.

As the number of aircraft in service built up, the engine behaviour in all respects improved. The RB 199 was highly competitive with contemporary US products, and had the multi-role characteristics demanded by Tornado which no alternative engine could have provided.

Conclusions

While the final production standard engine has provided satisfactory reliability and performance, the programme incurred greater engineering effort than originally planned with a consequent increase in development costs. The following comments identify the adverse factors.

    a. The historical background, the consequences of the merger of the two UK engine companies, and the need to evolve collaborative

relationships as the programme proceeded, resulted in some immaturity of the design as originally committed to production.
b. The engine programme was not launched until after the commencement of airframe design. It is accepted that mature engines cannot be made available at the start of flight testing unless the full engine development programme is started at least two years ahead of the airframe.
c. The launch was not preceded by the running of a demonstrator engine and rig test components could not be acquired sufficiently in advance of full engine testing.
d. The political circumstances preceding the launch and, in particular, the competition phase forced the commitment to ambitious performance standards with few reserves or margins to cope with emerging difficulties.

Footnote
Demonstration of an uprated RB 199 was made in anticipation of a requirement arising for the fighter version of Tornado. In the event this option was not taken up.

Engine design studies accurately predicted the European Fighter requirement and enabled a relevant demonstrator engine and component rigs to be built and tested well in advance of the full programme launch. This effectively conferred a lead of four years relative to the RB 199 timescale. Nevertheless the first EFA was initially flown with RB 199 engines, removing the distraction to the programme of the need for very early flight development engines. Ironically, this process, while fully meeting the objectives set, has not resulted in the predicted cost saving due to extension of the timescale by the customer nations.

TORNADO IDS AVIONIC SYSTEM
Peter Hearne

Peter Hearne graduated from Cranfield in 1949 and spent ten years with BOAC and BEA on the development of operating techniques for helicopters and gas turbine aircraft. He joined Elliott Brothers, later GEC Marconi, in 1959 and led the development of digital equipment for a wide variety of advanced military aircraft from the TSR2 through the Jaguar and Tornado to all variants of the F-16 and even some 'friendly' MiG-21s. He retired as Chairman of GEC Avionics in 1994 having served previously as Assistant Managing Director of the GEC Marconi group. He has over 4,500 hours in the air with multi-engine and instrument ratings and also holds a Diamond C gliding badge.

Introduction

When Jock Heron asked me to speak on the Tornado avionic system he asked me, like the BBC Panel Game to talk for fifteen minutes 'without hesitation, repetition or deviation.' My first thought was 'What a pity that the Tornado programme itself did not follow the same rules!'

The Tornado system was the follow-on evolution of the then classic British preference for the low level penetrator strike aircraft. It took the concept pioneered on the TSR2, and cut down on the single-seat Jaguar, added a powerful mapping and Terrain Following Radar, restored the back seater/system operator and added a substantial RWR/EW system. It evolved from the all-weather nuclear capability of TSR2, through the VMC conventional/nuclear role of the Jaguar, towards an all-weather conventional and nuclear capability against pre-planned targets.

Jock has told me that he and his OR colleagues had a difficult time getting the balance right between the rapidly evolving capabilities of digital and other types of avionics and the need to establish realistic requirements which did not push the system so far that it became impractical to realise. On the whole I think they got it right, though possibly with a little too much caution brought about by that other all-powerful new ingredient the 'collaboration factor' which tends to favour the lowest common denominator.

System Design and Integration

It is impossible to talk about Tornado without recognising the major influences, not always good, which collaboration played in the choice and evolution of design solutions. At the starting gate it was apparent that a system of this complexity and with this number of players would require a powerful and effective system integration team. This team's task would be: to prepare an effective top-down system design to meet the requirement; subsequently to partition this into closely controlled technical and purchasing specifications; and eventually conducting or helping to conduct the integration and proving and flight tests.

In the TSR2 programme this team had been the System Integration Group at Vickers, headed by Howard Surtees supported by Frank Bond and John Daboo. This team had now migrated *en bloc* to form ESAMS a totally and fiercely independent system integrator though owned by Elliott's. Because of the collaborative nature of the programme German and Italian input was politically important and a group known as ESG was formed headed by ESAMS. At the time the imposition of this independent systems team seemed to the avionic system suppliers to be a major hindrance. In retrospect it was obviously essential in a tri-national programme and I am happy to pay tribute to the excellence of their achievement.

Two of their first tasks were to design the architecture of the computing system and to establish a digital data transmission system, both being important drivers which had been identified during TSR2 development. Fortunately with this background there was little difficulty in seeing off a German initiative led by IBM (Germany) to put *all* of the system functions, autopilot, engine control, wing sweep, stores management, etc into a single computer, which they reluctantly admitted might have to be duplicated for reliability. A federated system based on individual system-dedicated computers was chosen, a concept which emerged strongly from BAC's and Elliott's TSR2 experience.

More difficult was the selection of a data transmission system which was a choice between a multiplex data bus ring highway and a 'star' dedicated link system between individual boxes and the centre. The Americans were in the process of finalising the MIL STD 1553 system which was the forerunner of a series of successful ring highway systems which have greatly reduced interface complexity and, *most importantly*, have greatly simplified the process of retrofitting upgraded or changed sensors and sub-systems. The 'star' system was similar in concept to the digital data transmission system then being evolved for the new 747/DC-10 series of civil aircraft. It also represented substantial, but smaller, weight and cost savings but traded off lower technical risk *now* against substantially increased difficulty in retrofit/upgrades in the future.

The later Tornado GR4 would undoubtedly have been easier, cheaper and earlier if a 1553 system had been chosen initially and the addition of TIALD would have been much simpler. Having worked with both systems, I would today have no hesitation in saying MIL 1553 was to be preferred. But in 1970/71 it would undoubtedly have been a substantially high risk solution to chose MIL 1553 which, like GPS - and Skybolt - was totally controlled by the USA. The 'star' system has performed satisfactorily over time and is now complemented in the aircraft by ring highway bus systems.

The Equipment Selection Process

The detailed specifications for the ESAMS/ESG eventually made their way, via NAMMA and Panavia, through the three aircraft contractors to the equipment manufacturers. After the bids were submitted the selection process began, conducted by an organisation comprising national representatives of the three countries, together with ESG and Panavia personnel, known as the QCP (Equipment Control Panel). This was an organisation as much like a Medici or Borgia court as it was a dedicated technical evaluation group and I am afraid that it had to be, because, to the equipment manufacturers, its main objective seemed to be a policy of 'select equipment vendors, as far as possible, which optimise the industrial workshare participation with the least harmful effect on the aircraft's operational capability.' You can vary the emphasis you put on these two factors but workshare and specification compliance were *always* the main balancing act in equipment selection.

The process was obviously flawed by the fact that Germany and Germans tried to solve in most instances by relying on importing US equipment, eg radar, for their share which, at that time, was frowned on by the consortium rules.

At the start of the process the big ticket items lined up as:
    a. The Germans wanted the J-Band mapping radar; the X-Band TF package (from Texas Instruments, derived from the F-111 radar); the Litton (Germany) IN and/or mission computer and, if possible, the Flight Control System as well.

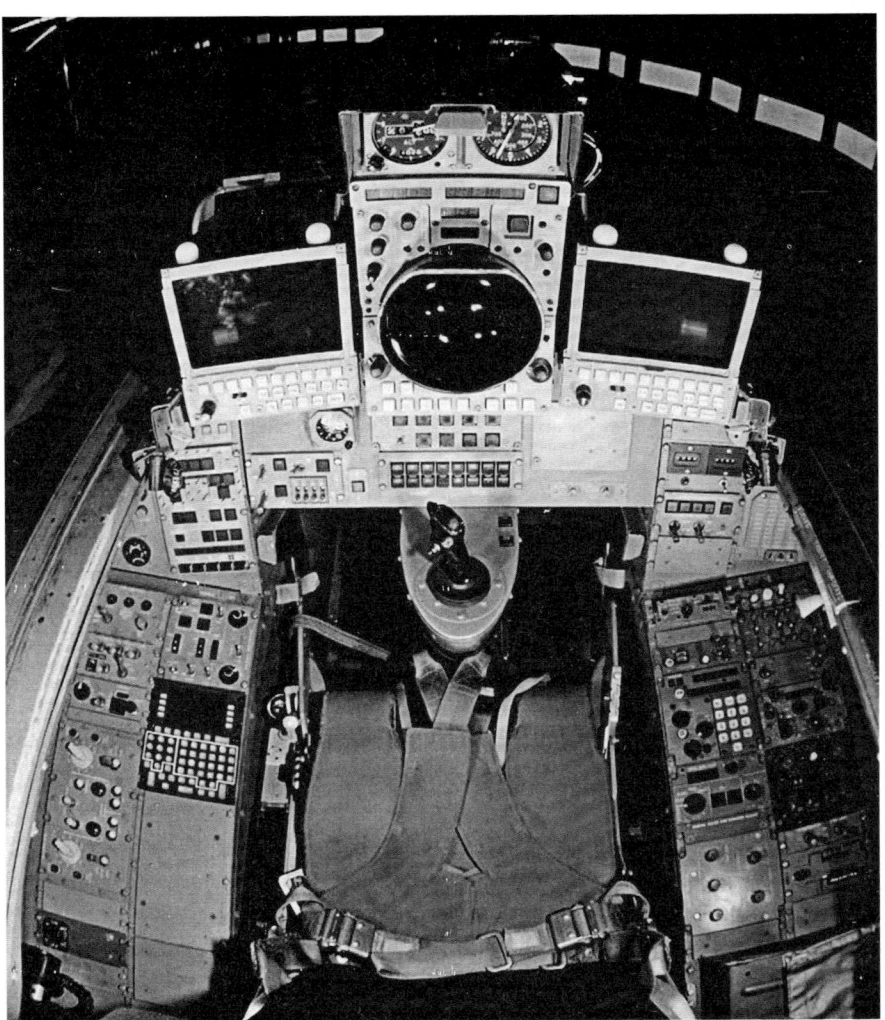
Rear cockpit of a Tornado GR 4.

b. The UK Government desperately wanted the Ferranti IN platform, which was a good bit of kit at the time of selection and one into which a great deal of UK Government money had been sunk. They also wanted the Elliott Fly-By-Wire/CSAS/autopilot which was an evolution of the TSR2 Flight Control System.

c. The UK had also proposed a very innovative Ferranti/Elliott-conceived dual band Q/X radar system with a single larger diameter antenna which, it was claimed/hoped, would considerably improve the resolution of the mapping radar for blind attack. They also supported a UK computer selection with some bias towards the Elliott 920 ATC which was a 128k machine (later evolved to 250k) already in hand for the Nimrod Mk 2 sonar with strong in-service software support and provenance from the earlier 920 series computers in the Jaguar and the Nimrod Mk 1.

What actually happened was:

Good Buys

The American Texas Instruments (TI) radar package was selected with AEG as principal European contractor. It has been very successful and should be counted as one of the better, or even the best, purchasing decisions. The Ferranti/Elliott system would certainly have been longer in timescale and probably more expensive. It would ultimately have given a better blind attack radar imaging capability for most, but not all, weather conditions and thus an increased capability against smaller fixed and mobile targets.

The UK's Ferranti IN platform was selected. While this had an excellent performance capability at the time, it had the longer term effect of stifling the introduction of non-floated gyros, and later laser gyros, into UK service. This was not the intention, as Ferranti had hoped to upgrade the system with a laser gyro system at the Mid Life Update, but UK funding politics got in the way at the time when the Product Improvement Policy could have been introduced.

There appeared to have been, at least an indication of, horse trading between the choice of a primary US/German radar contractor and a sole UK source for the IN.

The Elliott FBW CSAS and digital autopilot was selected and has proved successful in service with surprisingly few problems. A Spin Prevention System and later a digital version for the ADV were subsequently added. A criticism has been voiced that the system is too successful in modifying, and hence suppressing, the tell tale signs of change of handling characteristics with aircraft stores loadings and weight, something which we should take note of for the future.

In the UK, Smiths provided a good HUD as well as a very necessary computer interface unit to match Litton's computer and much effective electronic housekeeping and control systems for the basic airframe system such as electrical generation.

In Italy Microtechnica in the north provided a very high quality source of complex mechanical engineering assemblies whilst Selenia in the south had a surprisingly advanced and wide ranging input on the technologies on many of the electronics systems.

Good Tries

The Litton (Germany) computer Spirit II was selected. An inoffensive computer which has met its rather limited specification but has required considerable updating and is a bit of an orphan, with no ancestors and few descendants, which limits the opportunity for cross fertilisation of new ideas.

There was a widespread belief that radar fixing accuracy would be improved if we could provide an overall area match of radar returns, instead of relying on single designated points which might not turn out to be radar prominent. Sadly, this idea did not turn out so well, partly due to stretch in the map film, but also because area radar returns are not necessarily more accurately correlated with the map than are single radar prominences.

Interestingly when Marconi-Elliott flew a full up Terrain Reference Navigation system in an A-6 hack aircraft, which was an early A-12 system demonstrator, over the Blue Ridge Mountains the radar map match against a digital electronic map showed the same type of problems.

In passing I would comment that the advent of accurate Terrain Reference Navigation, even without GPS aiding, suggests that the specifications of Forward Looking Radars in future strike aircraft (if any) could change radically - particularly with the elimination of the Terrain Following Radar which seems now to have the same lethal potential as the use of IFF by Bomber Command over Germany in 1943/44.

Good Grief

Two man-made black holes (there were probably more), were the Stores Management System and the Automatic Test Equipment both, I'm sorry to say, within my general orbit. The Stores Management System suffered from the fact that its main design requirements did *not* seem to centre around the need to select and get weapons off the aircraft quickly, as required in the heat and stress of battle. Instead, a large amount of the complexity lay in preventing the inadvertent release of conventional weapons (which had, in the past, annoyed some of the voters in Scotland) and in the dreaded weapons package system which always seemed to me to be a solution looking for an unlikely problem. The fact that the initial programme had to be abandoned and that the Germans went their own way with a different system is compelling evidence of a faulty concept. As I understand it, this split and the lack of commonality on bomb slips may have helped to destroy a lot of the much wanted interoperability between different air forces. I believe Eurofighter has not been immune from this disease.

Those of you who have flown the F-16, with its much simpler attack switch moding, in which the operation of a safe Stores Management System is integrated with the overall mission system and controlled in large part from switches on the throttle and stick, will, I think, realise that we need to change our design priorities and requirements management in this area.

Automatic Test Equipment was a self inflicted wound of immense magnitude on the part of NAMMA/Panavia, even though all of the evidence necessary to avoid it was available at the start of the programme. The US Navy had shown that one very effective way of providing a value-for-money ATE, which minimised test software costs and limited the spread of special test equipment, was to define, at the start of a major aircraft programme, standard electronic/electrical and mechanical test interface characteristics that every prime equipment manufacturer should meet. If the prime equipment was so uniquely wonderful that it couldn't fit in with the standard ATE interface then the prime equipment won selection marks for magic performance, but lost selection marks for supportability, and vice versa. This strategy results in a much simpler and more cost effective effort to produce test software. This simple solution was available to, and strongly recommended by, Elliott's to the Tornado programme management team on Day 1 with the further endorsement that they had to make up their mind on ATE strategy in a timely manner; this they did not do. Instead, NAMMA/Panavia dithered and dallied and lost their way and didn't know where to go, with the result that the cost and effort in writing and re-writing test software was at one time threatening to impact the future of the whole aircraft programme.

Fortunately, with much better BITE/Self Test capabilities now readily available in the aircraft equipment itself, we should not have to make this mistake again but beware.

I have put Digital Engine Control on this list but I will only comment that the delays in this area did not stem from programme management but more from the inherent conservatism of the engine consortium.

In Conclusion

The final result has been a new attack system whose built-in flexibility, by design and not by chance, has enabled it to accommodate quite radical changes in tactical weapons over its long service life.

And finally, a good friend of mine, the late Peter Harrison, whilst in an AD slot in the Future Systems cell of MOD PE(AIR) wrote a paper which suggested that, on the basis of Tornado experience, a wholly national programme for AST403 (now Eurofighter) would be no more expensive, and certainly much quicker, than a collaborative one. Needless to say, this paper was quickly suppressed in Whitehall and Peter was 'asked' to re-issue it with a markedly different conclusion.

However, when I look at the UK-industry funded Experimental Aircraft Programme (EAP) prototype, now languishing for over ten years in a university museum of all places, since the end of its successful flying programme, it proves, I think, that he had quite a lot of right on his side.

Global collaboration seems to be a present day imperative to reduce costs, much of which, however, are self-fulfilling and self-inflicted and are created *by* the elaborate management and decision structures which become necessary in such complex collaboration programmes and in which the delays (particularly in decision making), elapsed times, and hence costs, usually go up, sometimes exponentially.

I would like to suggest that on some future occasion the RAFHS might care to consider the RAF's past experience on collaborative programmes to see whether they can draw some conclusions which would enable us to concentrate on the good features and remove, as far as possible, the bad features of these types of venture.

To summarise, I would highlight the following salient points from the overall Tornado programme:

1. Very successful systems definition by ESAMS/ESG, with excellent flexibility and growth.
2. Most equipment is satisfactory and the system did meet its specification.
3. Some black holes but due to human, rather than structural, defects in system design.

4. Arbitrary work sharing (as opposed to work sharing for proven technical or time scale advantages) is the enemy of cost, time and technical advance.

The end product.

THE MUNICH SCENE
Alan Thornber

Alan Thornber joined English Electric as an engineering apprentice in 1947 and worked on the Canberra before fulfilling an extended RAF National Service commitment as an engineer. He returned to Warton in 1959 to work first on the Lightning and TSR2 programmes and then in supply management for the Jaguar project. In 1969 he was assigned to Panavia in Munich and was for over ten years Director of Procurement eventually becoming Deputy Managing Director in 1981. He returned to Warton in 1987 as Director of Contracts – Military Aircraft, retiring five years later after filling a variety of Board-level appointments for both Panavia and Eurofighter.

Introduction

Organisation and administration are, in themselves, hardly likely to generate the sort of excitement which one might associate with devising a successful engineering solution to a given operational requirement. Nevertheless, satisfactory organisational arrangements were absolutely essential to the ultimate success of the Tornado programme. In many cases, the management procedures which evolved began with a clean sheet of paper, in much the same way as a specification or drawing, and it should be said that the application of these procedures was not always free from raised emotions! It did, however, provide for the establishment of common terms, conditions and management procedures which became internationally accepted across the entire programme.

The 'Munich Scene' evolved largely as a result of the customer nations' need for a central management organisation having the necessary expertise and authority to be able to direct the project through a single-point-of-contact joint industrial company. The latter was to be fully accountable and capable of providing appropriate contract performance guarantees for each phase of the programme. In short, the aim was to have 'single prime contractor responsibility'.

By the late 1960s there had already been several collaborative programmes involving a variety of management arrangements. It is not my intention to suggest that the management arrangements devised for the Tornado should necessarily represent the blueprint for all collaborative programmes but I will say that they were created as a result of some far sighted initial policy directives, and that they were sustained by a very real desire on the part of all those involved to make the programme the success that it was.

Before looking more closely at some of the specific procedures which were established to manage the programme it would be appropriate to consider some of the events which preceded the launch of the Definition Phase and which had a particular impact on the subsequent management arrangements for the programme.

The Lead-In To The Definition Phase

By mid July 1968 six nations had signed a Memorandum of Understanding (MOU) which would initiate a Concept Feasibility Phase which was to run until April 1969, the object being to undertake studies aimed at satisfying the requirements of MRA-75.

By December 1968 the four nations remaining in the programme had established an Interim Management Organisation (IMO) located in Munich which acted as a focal point for inter-government dialogue and contact with industry.

On 26th March 1969 a Joint Industrial Company Collaboration Agreement had been ratified. This marked the formation of Panavia Aircraft GmbH which was to be collocated with the IMO in Munich. By the time that the Definition Phase of the programme was launched in May 1969 the four nations had also agreed to set up NAMMO/NAMMA. NAMMA was formally established alongside Panavia in Munich on 1st September 1969.

Overall Programme

Throughout the programme, control over the authorisation of work was exercised in the first instance by inter-governmental MOUs (see Figure 1) covering predetermined significant aspects of the programme, each MOU requiring the formal approval of the participating nations.

Covered by these MOUs, NAMMA was able to authorise the contractual work packages to industry. For those elements of the programme covering the period prior to flight of the prototype some nine individual MOUs were introduced, one of the most important being

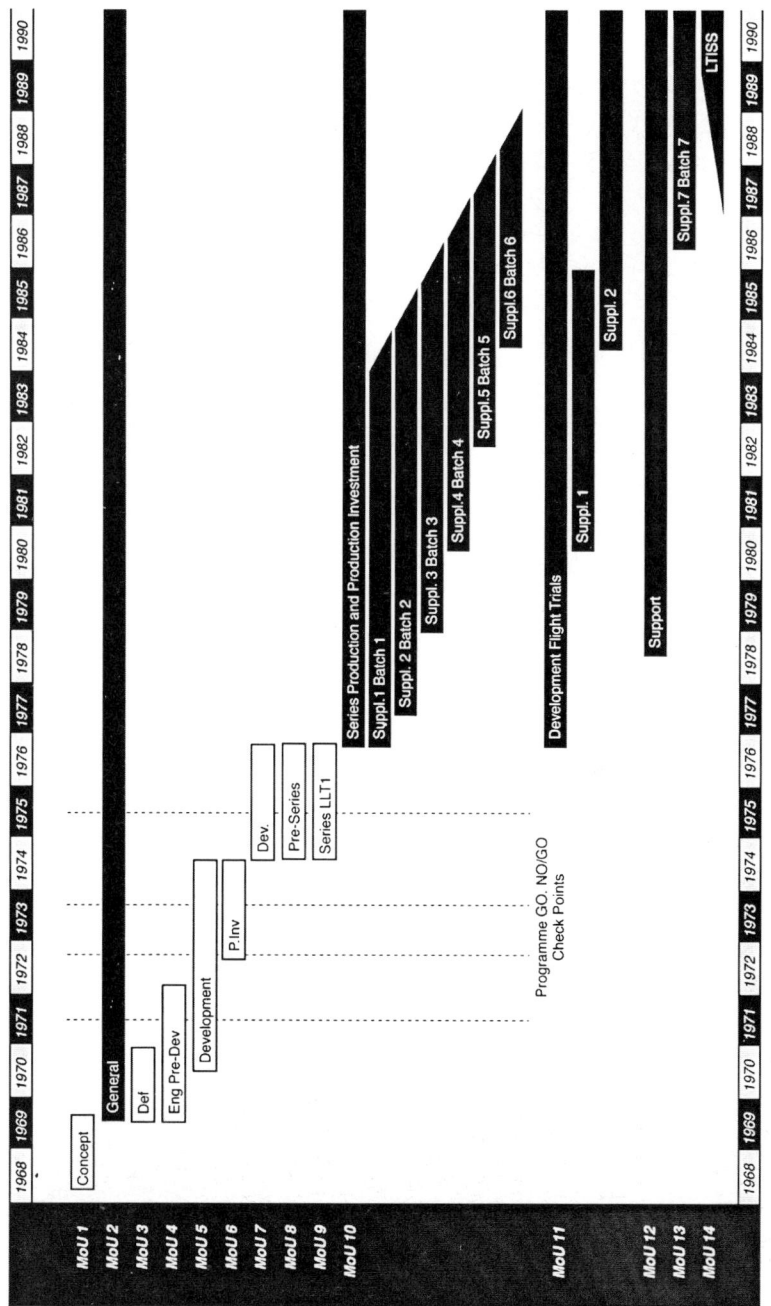

Fig 1. Intergovernmental MOUs

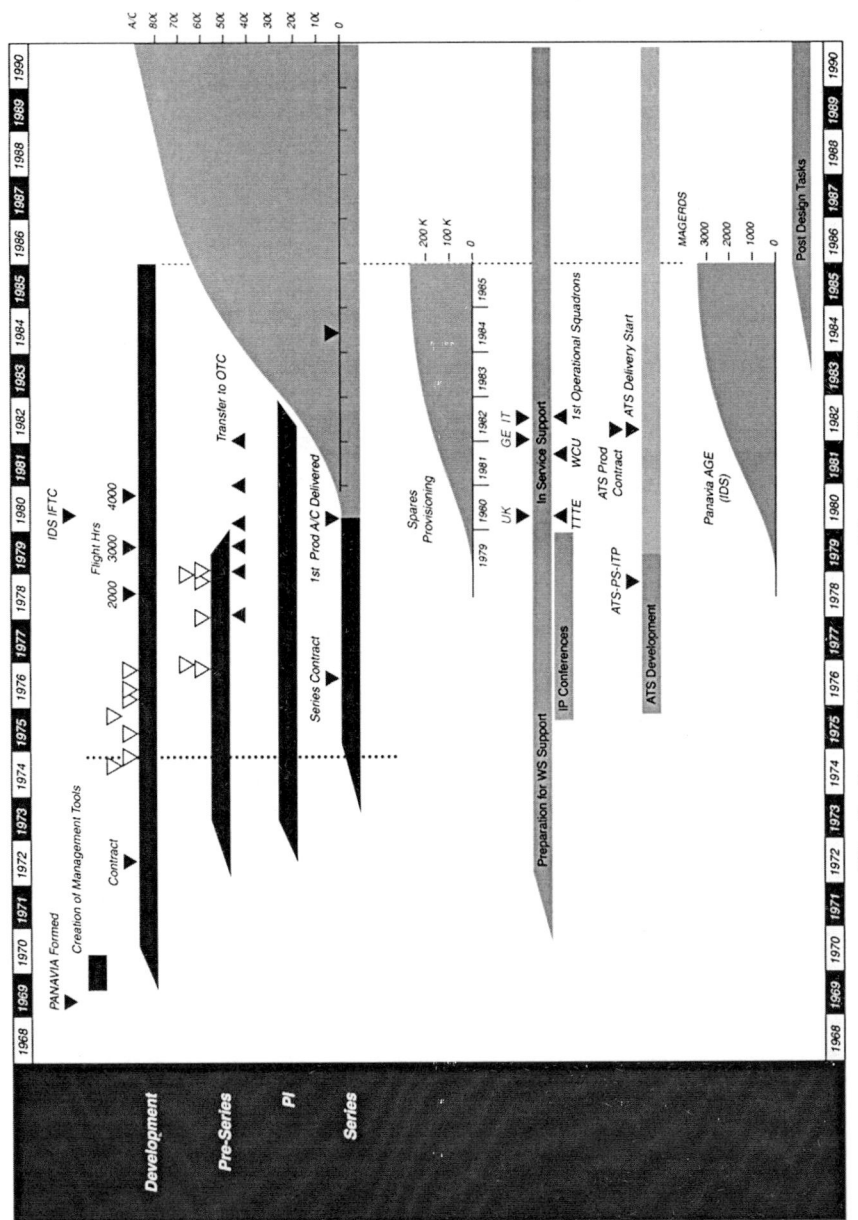

Fig 2. Overall Programme Phasing Chart.

MOU 2 which, in effect, was the enabling agreement from which other all other MOUs were derived.

Of particular interest was the creation of a number of programme Go/No Go check points each of which provided the individual nations with an opportunity to withdraw from the programme without threat of compensation penalty.

To ensure the smooth build up of industrial resources in anticipation of future production needs, it was necessary to ensure that there is a measure of 'phase overlap' within the programme (see Figure 2) and it is notable that Long Lead Time Item (LLTI) release for series production was coincident with the flight of the first two prototypes.

The autumn of 1974, when these significant events took place, may therefore be regarded as one of the major milestones in the Tornado programme. This was the stage at which the aspirations and optimism of those involved in the programme began to make way for the reality of actual development aircraft taking to the air, this being coupled with formal series production authorisation by the three governments.

Organisation

Turning now to the customer organisation, during the course of 1968 each of the nations involved had been providing the necessary specialist support for meetings and discussions to further the aims of the international Joint Working Group (JWG), most of these arrangement having been organised on an *ad hoc* basis. By the end of the year, however, it had became clear that more formal procedures would have to be established in order to co-ordinate the views of the individual nations. What was needed was an internationally staffed body which could express these views to industry while providing an official forum for debate. This requirement was satisfied by the IMO which was set up in Munich on the 15th December 1968. It was headed by a Dutch Air Force general with an RAF air commodore (Ray Watts) as his deputy. Key functional areas of the programme were handled by specialist cells staffed by senior national representatives, the five main functional areas being Military Factors, Engineering/Technical, Finance, Contracts, Plans and Programmes.

Until it was superseded by NAMMA in September 1969, the IMO was responsible for formalising the authorisation of all activities of the

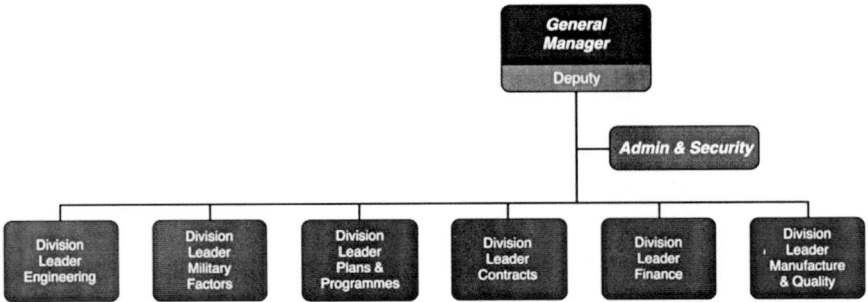

Fig 3. NAMMA – Management Organisation (end 1972).

programme on behalf of the nations through the issue of directives to industry and the negotiation of associated contractual cover to allow further studies to be carried out by industry.

The formation of NAMMA, as the customer nations' authorised 'agency', provided a more permanent and broader management structure, although it continued to reflect the same main functional areas that had been defined by the IMO (see Figure 3). Furthermore, in many cases, the key national personnel assigned to the IMO remained in post in Munich but now having NATO status. In fact NAMMA functioned on very similar lines to that of the earlier IMO, albeit it was somewhat larger, staff levels having been increased to handle the increased workload. By the end of 1972 NAMMA's strength in personnel was comparable to that of the industrial organisation, Panavia.

In parallel with the activities of the Government authorities, the industrial organisations nominated by each of the nations had been providing specialist support and interface throughout 1968 and early 1969. On 26th March 1969 the four industrial concerns, BAC, Fiat, Fokker and MBB, formed a partnership under a formal Collaboration Agreement. This agreement also provided the necessary Memorandum of Association for the creation of a jointly owned company, Panavia Aircraft GmbH, with its principle place of business in Munich and subject to German Law.

The agreement also prescribed in detail the manner in which the joint company should operate and provided for an organisation representing the four Partner Company Shareholders. By late 1972 the allocation of

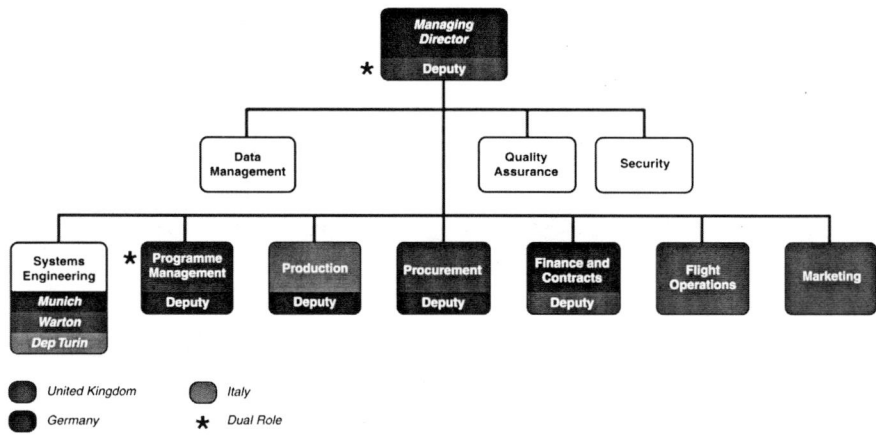

Fig 4. Panavia Aircraft Gmbh Organisation Chart, 1972.

key posts to senior partner company personnel within the central Panavia organisation (from which the Netherlands had now withdrawn) was in direct proportion to the work sharing levels dictated by the number of production aircraft on order for each customer nation. Six of the functional Director or Deputy Director positions at Munich were therefore filled by Panavia-assigned managers from BAC; another six were on assignment from MBB, whilst Fiat provided the remaining two (as indicated at Figure 4). Such a distribution provided the closest practical relationship to the Panavia shareholder and worksharing ratios of 42.5% UK (BAC), 42.5% Germany (MBB) and 15% Italy (Fiat). The total numbers of staff within Panavia at the end of 1972, inclusive of locally employed supporting personnel, was approaching 150 as compared with the initial 1969-70 staffing level of around 60.

The collaboration agreement formally introduced very significant and far reaching policy directives which resulted directly from the requirements of the four nations that there must be a legally established single joint company to take the responsibility for the programme, in other words to act as prime contractor. This is clearly reflected in the constitution of Panavia and it provided the framework for all of Panavia's future direction and management. The key statement was as follows:

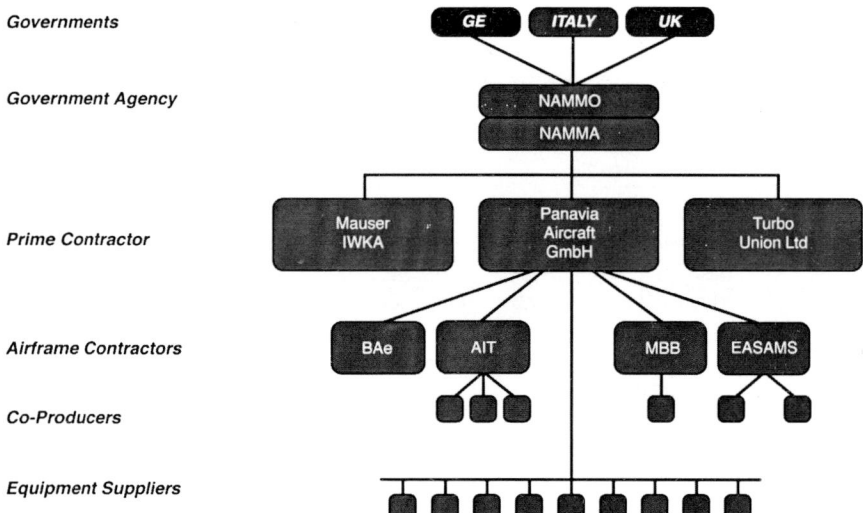

Fig 5. *Tornado Contractual Structure – Development Phase*

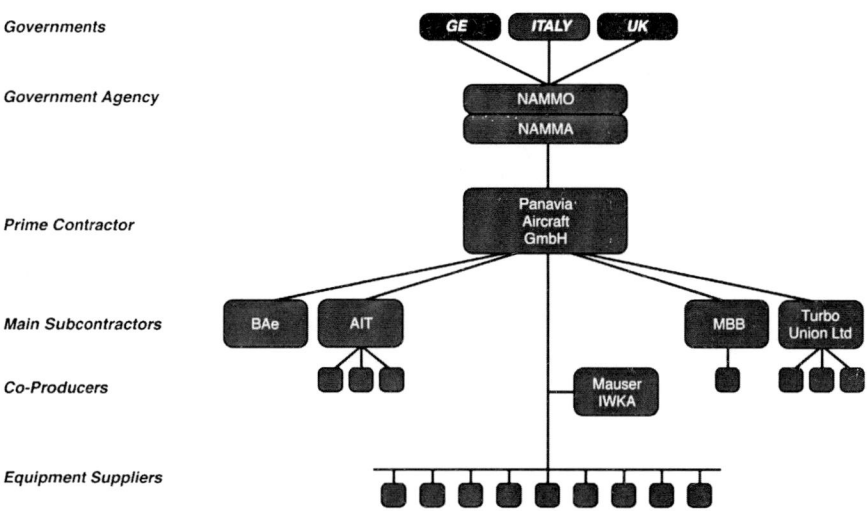

Fig 6. *Tornado Contractual Structure – Production Phase*

'The Joint Company shall be the sole agency for the receipt and administration of contracts relating to the aircraft Programme and for submitting reports, proposals, offers, quotations, and other technical and commercial documentation to customer. Panavia shall have management and control responsibility for the Aircraft Programme and it shall be responsible for the placing of related subcontracts to the Participants or to any other party.'

The central management organisation was therefore tasked:-

- To co-ordinate the management of the design, initial build and full production of the complete MRCA system.
- To contract directly for the aircraft and for avionics development.
- To control all equipment purchasing.
- To undertake all reporting to, and negotiation with, customer agencies.
- To administer configuration control and quality assurance and arrange marketing and public relations.

In practice, the contractual structure for the Development Phase of the programme acknowledged a special relationship which the customer directed should exist between himself and the respective companies responsible for the engine and the gun (see Figure 5). By contrast, for the Production Phase, the contractual structure was routed via the single prime contractor, albeit with strong national governmental influences (see Figure 6)

The primary government/industry interface for the Tornado programme was based on the executive 'agencies', NAMMA and Panavia, (see Figure 7) which were collocated in a single building at Arrabellastrasse 16-24, an address that became very familiar to the many representatives from national government agencies, air forces and industrial contractors who had reason to visit over the years, to present their views and to express their opinions.

The Munich Scene

Following the signature of the Collaboration Agreement in March 1969, the first Board of Directors meeting took place at Weybridge on 17th

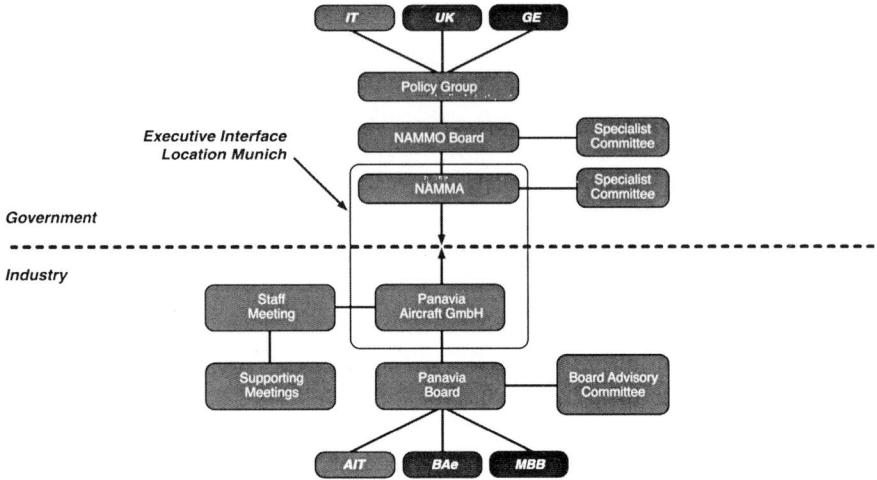

Fig 7. Government/Industry Interface.

April. Allen Greenwood of BAC was appointed Chairman of the Board for a period of two years with Ludwig Bölkow as Deputy Chairman. At the same meeting Gero Madelung was appointed Managing Director of Panavia Aircraft GmbH, a position he was to hold, and from where he successfully directed the industrial programme, until 1978.

It is perhaps of interest to note that the 1969 Collaboration Agreement identified the aircraft as 'the Panther (or such other name as may be agreed by the Participants) multi role combat weapon system'. It was not until early 1976 that the name Tornado was formally introduced.

Key Government/Industry Interface Issues

The contractually funded Programme Management System provided the main vehicle by which a regular and extremely comprehensive level of programme information, and progress against planned events, was reported by industry to the customer through the Panavia/NAMMA network. There were a number of issues and procedures where there would, at times, be constant and intense dialogue, and it may be appropriate to highlight a number of these key Government/Industry Interface issues.

Equipment Tendering and Selection - The Equipment Control Panel (QCP)

One has only to look at the relationship of the major elements of the flyaway price of a production aircraft to recognise that the equipment element represents a major slice of the overall costs. The engine and gun cost approximately 25%; the airframe costs 37% with equipment making up the remaining 38%.

Whereas in an aircraft project prior to the MRCA a significant proportion of the major equipments would be provided free of charge to the main contractor on a 'government furnished' basis, on this programme there would be initially no GFE and the responsibility for supply was to rest with the prime contractor. In consideration of this, and bearing in mind the considerable number of equipment specialists resident in national government establishments, it did not come as a complete surprise to realise that the customer would need a voice in the selection of both the equipment and its suppliers.

The IMO had given considerable attention to this matter during 1969 and there had been many discussions with representation from Panavia on the practicalities involved. A directive issued by NAMMA in September 1969 identified the governmental requirements by defining the 'Principles Governing Equipment Selection and Procedures'. Amongst other things the directive prescribed that 'the governments of the participating countries will be consulted during the process of selection to enable them, where they wish, to approve, or to propose amendments to, the terms of the specification, the list of firms invited to tender and the proposed choice of contractor'.

This resulted in the formation of a body known as the Equipment Control Panel, the QCP, through which all equipment matters were to be channelled. This institution, chaired by NAMMA, provided a means whereby national specialists could express their views.

At that time it was anticipated that there would be in excess of 350 individual Panavia specified equipments to be dealt with. The major items, those with so-called Category B status, would have the most significant government involvement.

Governmental involvement via the QCP led to a timescale of at least thirty weeks from the initial specification being prepared by Panavia to the selection of a supplier for that equipment (see Figure 8). The formal selection process involved a very thorough assessment of suppliers'

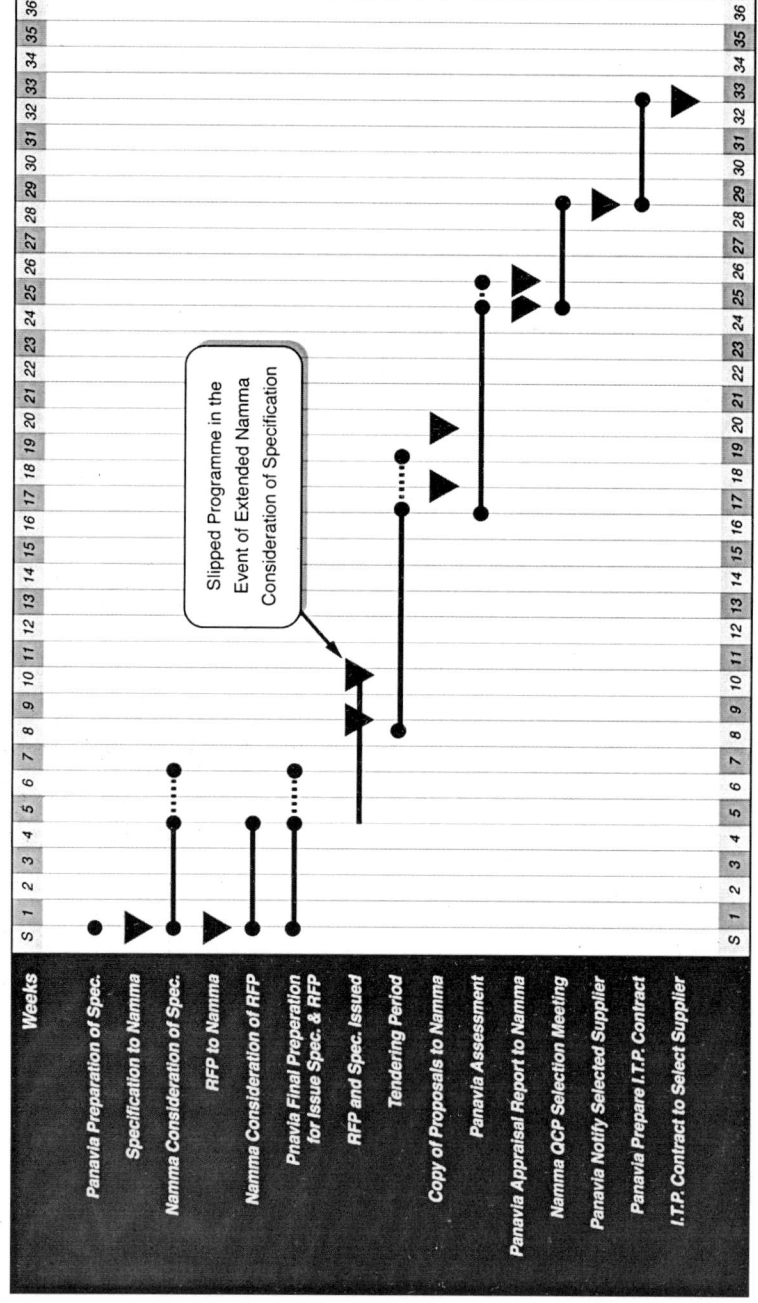

Fig 8. Timescale – Tendering and Selection of Category B Equipment

proposals and a very detailed and precise recording of analysis and decisions throughout.

In the case of Category B equipments NAMMA, and each of the Nations, would require at least four weeks to consider the contents of each drafted equipment specification and the associated tender documentation. As well as receiving copies of all the suppliers proposals, the nations would require at least four more weeks to study the Panavia appraisal reports of all the suppliers' proposals. Panavia was at that stage called upon to make a *single* recommendation to an assembled gathering of NAMMA and government specialists attending a selection meeting of the QCP.

There is no record of the QCP ever having turned down such a Panavia recommendation, although in a number of cases, it did impose a caveat calling for some readjustment of the worksharing balance of work between the three participating countries. Nevertheless, on many of the major equipments a level of worksharing was put forward which would allow work to be performed in each of arrangements involving a particular item which led, in turn, to further discussions. The radar was such a special case, with Panavia being called upon to conduct parallel negotiations, with both Texas Instruments and Autonetics, over fully initialled contractual documentation before coming forward with a single recommendation.

The processes of tendering for, and the selection of equipment suppliers for, those 350 items resulted in the QCP being in almost continuous session throughtout 1970-72. There is no doubt that the development programme suffered delays as a result of the protracted equipment supplier selection procedure. On the other hand, the nature of the task is such, particularly on an international collaborative programme, that the selection process has not only to be scrupulously fair; it has also to be clearly *seen* to be fair.

Worksharing

The customer nations, having determined that the overall sharing of work within the participating countries should be apportioned in the ratio of the numbers of production aircraft to be ordered by each nation, it was left to industry to formulate plans for the implementation of this requirement. In so far as the airframe was concerned there was agreement from the very early days of the programme for the design and manufacture of the constituent parts to be undertaken as follows:

- Fiat (Alenia) would be be responsible for the wings.
- BAC (BAE Systems) would be responsible for front and rear fuselage, fin and tailerons.
- MB (EADS) would be responsible for the centre fuselage.

Three final assembly lines would be introduced but single-source manufacture of component parts would be the order of the day. As far as the equipment was concerned the situation was rather more complex.

Although equipment suppliers were encouraged to submit proposals for the sharing of work it was often neither practical nor cost effective for such worksharing arrangements to be implemented. In many cases a solo development/single-source manufacturer was far and away the best solution, although the natural process of selection over an increasing number of equipments did serve to create some balance of work between the three participating countries. Nevertheless, on many of the major equipments a level of worksharing was put forward which would allow work to be performed in each of the three countries strictly on the basic of solo development/single source manufacture and in a manner best suited to the skills and experience of the companies involved. In all cases, the nomination of a lead contractor was mandatory. An analysis of worksharing across some 325 specific equipments indicates that 175 contracts went to UK suppliers, 126 to German companies, seventeen to the Italians and seven to other nations.

In monetary terms (related to May 1970 economic conditions) the sharing of work reflected targets established by the QCP and the Panavia equipment selection process. The agreed proportions were 42.5% UK, 32.5% Germany; 12.4% Italy, 0.9% other nations and 11.7% transferred *in* to Europe. The latter figure refers specifically to the radar system of which the first 218 units were manufactured by Texas Instruments. Through a Technical Transfer Agreement, manufacture of the 219th and subsequent systems was undertaken by a European consortium headed by AEG with a 49% German, 25% British and 26% Italian work distribution.

Panavia was responsible for providing ongoing worksharing arrangements across the programme with verification being provided through the accumulation of claims and expenditure expressed in the currencies of the countries where the work was undertaken.

On the basis of the data submitted, the customer was responsible for carrying out any necessary harmonisation of the overall workshare requirements.

Pricing - Cost Control - Payment Arrangements

One of the most exacting tasks which the central organisation was called upon to perform was the compilation of the very comprehensive cost proposals which had to pull together the estimated cost of activities throughout the participating nations and beyond.

The viability of a programme as large as the Tornado project is critically dependent, not only on its affordability, but, just as importantly, on the ability of the participating nations to provide the flow of funding necessary to support that programme over time.

The initial price quotations covering Development Phase, Pre-Series and Series Production estimates were submitted in April 1970 and it is important to note that these were prepared to a baseline of May 1970 economic conditions and exchange rates relevant at that time.

Over the following years a tremendous amount of effort was necessary to reassure the customers that the estimates remained valid. Prior to each programme checkpoint and programme phased authorisation, the nations demanded an updated set of proposals with complete reconciliation back to the original estimates of 1970. Continued authorisation of programme funding was entirely dependent upon satisfactory acceptance by the customer nations of these updated cost proposals.

The success of these activities and of the cost control measures that went with them may best be demonstrated in the Development Programme by making a comparison of actual costs incurred up to the end of 1978 (de-escalated back to the cost estimates prepared in 1971 and Contractual Limits of Liability negotiated in 1972). See Figure 9.

On 21 September 1974, not long after the first flight of the prototype, MOD UK announced that total developments costs had amounted to £345M of which £166 million had been contributed by UK. This compared with an estimate of £114M made in 1970. The difference was accounted for by: inflation (£40M); devaluation of the pound against the Deutschmark (£2 M) and £8M for an increase in the UK's share following a reduction in the number of production aircraft required by

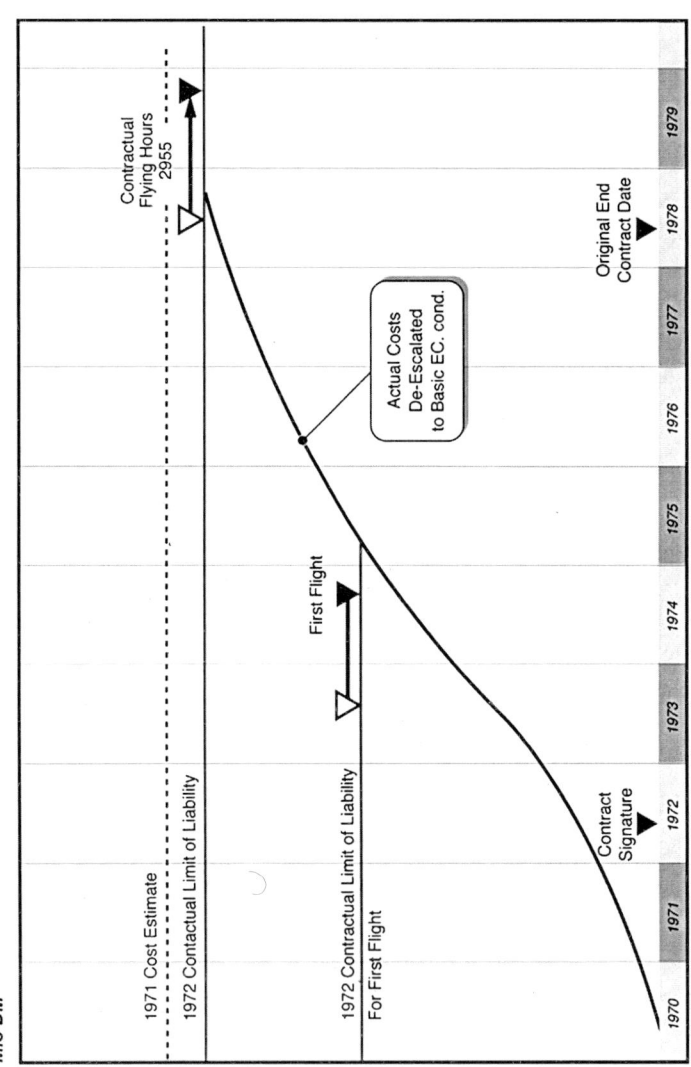

Fig 9. Development Phase Cost Comparison 1971-79.

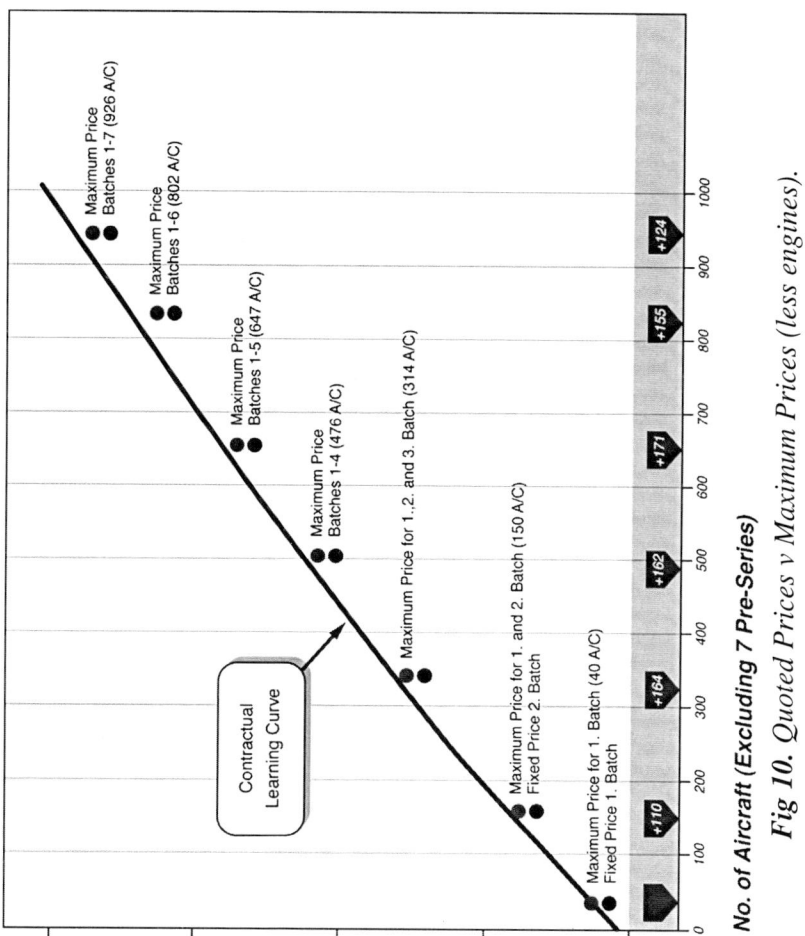

Fig 10. *Quoted Prices v Maximum Prices (less engines).*

Germany. *In summary, manhours and material estimates had remained stable within 2% of the original estimates prepared in 1970.*

In April 1975 Panavia was asked to submit maximum price proposals for the 805 series production aircraft. It can be demonstrated that, in every case, the prices negotiated for each batch built between 1975 and 1985 fell within the learning curve of the overall maximum price quoted in 1975 (see Figure 10). Furthermore a fixed definitive price was negotiated for each production batch whilst the aircraft within that batch were actually being built. In each and every case the agreed fixed price for that batch fell well within the corresponding maximum price which had been agreed earlier when considering like for like.

One of the principle policy requirements of the programme which emanated from the nations was that:

> 'Work performed in any one of the three participating countries will be paid for by funds made available directly from the government within whose country the work is being carried out.'

This very sensible demand was intended to minimise the amount of money which might otherwise have been expended on currency transactions. In practical terms, this did call for some rather ingenious payment arrangements, in order to maintain centralised control of commitment and authorisation whilst allowing the money transfer, for example for equipment suppliers, to be carried out within national boundaries.

In conclusion I refer you back to my opening remarks where I said that it was not my intention to cite the arrangements which were set up to manage the Tornado programme as necessarily being the model for all future collaborative programmes. Nevertheless, from my personal involvement in the programme, for well over twenty years, I have no doubt that the management arrangements, from the government authorities through to the industrial participants, worked and worked very well. There are others who would agree with me. For instance, in 1974, Mr Brynmoor John, then the Under Secretary of State for the RAF, stated that 'It has been a splendid achievement to keep so close to the original estimates of cost and time', and a year later he said that 'The MRCA is clearly the most successful international collaboration ever, in which the real escalation of costs has been minimal and has been carefully controlled.'

Then again, the House of Commons Sixth Report of the Committee of Public Accounts (Session 1986/87, relating to the Control and Management of Major Equipment) attributes the following statement to Peter Levine on 15th December 1986:

> 'If you look at the Tornado, it is an excellent example of how to do these things properly and we expect and hope that the new European Fighter Aircraft will follow in its footsteps.'

But perhaps that is a story for another day!

Acknowledgements
My thanks to BAE SYSTEMS and Panavia Aircraft GmbH for their support and assistance in the preparation of material for this paper.

Series production under way at Augsburg 1978.

DEVELOPMENT FLYING
Paul Millett

Paul Millett flew Fireflies from HMSs Ocean *and* Glory *during the Korean War before attending the 1958 ETPS Course and spending the rest of his time in uniform at Farnborough and Bedford. On leaving the Fleet Air Arm in 1964 he joined Hawker Siddeley as a Buccaneer test pilot. He moved to BAC in 1968 to become the Jaguar project test pilot, flying from both Istres and Warton. He later became Chief Test Pilot at Warton and, as project pilot for the MRCA, made the first flight of the prototype. As Director of Flight Operations at Warton he continued to fly the MRCA/Tornado until 1982. He finally retired in 1992 having spent the previous ten years as Chief Executive Saudi Arabia for British Aerospace.*

When I arrived at Warton at the beginning of 1968, the Tornado was still a paper aeroplane, although the design at that time did bear a strong relationship to what became in due course the final design. Since I was very much involved with the Jaguar, I kept only a watching brief on the initial birth pangs of the project. Since there was still no decision on whether the aircraft would have one or two seats, cockpit design was not an immediate priority.

By 1969, both Jimmy Dell, the Warton Chief Test Pilot, and myself were spending most of our time in France with the Jaguar, so the responsibility for pilot-aspects of the cockpit design of the aircraft was passed on to David Eagles.

When I became CTP at the end of 1970, I was even more involved in Jaguar work at both Warton and Istres, so I was happy to allow Dave to continue with his sterling work on MRCA as the design stabilised and cockpit details began to emerge. The cockpit area was unusually roomy for an aircraft of its type, for which the aircrew were very grateful, but it was still necessary to ensure that all of the switches, knobs and other controls were positioned where they would be most accessible and were ergonomically correct for their particular use. Cockpit design was part of Warton's area of responsibility and there was close liaison between the aircrew and the designers. Cockpit conferences were rather like the

Front cockpit of an early production Tornado GR 1

Tower of Babel in that, not only were the aircrew of the three manufacturers and the three Ministries of Defence represented, as well as the designers, but NAMMA and Panavia also had to have their say. The result could have been chaotic, but we devised a system by which the Warton aircrew, in conjunction with our designers, decided what we wanted to put where, then, prior to the cockpit conferences, discussed our thoughts with the RAF MOD aircrew. This produced a solid body of opinion with a united front and well thought-out arguments to present to the sixty-odd participants of the cockpit conferences.

One new cockpit control which in our experience was unique to the Tornado was the wing sweep lever, which we did not have difficulty in positioning in the cockpit, but there was some controversy regarding the sense in which it should move. The Warton aircrew felt strongly that the lever should move in the natural sense, that is forward to sweep the wings forward and aft to sweep them back. Another body of opinion thought that the wing sweep lever should operate like a throttle so that when the pilot wanted to go faster he would push the lever forward and the wings would sweep back. Dave Eagles and I arranged a visit to Upper Heyford to look at the F-111 cockpit and see how they had solved the problem. We were pleased to see that the wing sweep control operated in what we thought was the correct sense, and when one of the USAF aircrew told us that the lever had initially operated in the opposite sense, but had then had to be changed around at considerable expense, that clinched it for us.

When the aerodynamic design of the airframe was finalised, the performance parameters were fed into experimental simulators at the three main design establishments so that the aircrew could get a feel of how the aircraft might fly. We found that the first task was to get a similar aircraft represented on all three simulators rather than three aircraft with a family resemblance to each other, but with some different characteristics. Each of the simulator engineers was certain that their version was the right one, but they did slowly converge until all three were sensibly the same aircraft. When we came to fly the real thing, I was pleased to note that it most closely resembled the Warton version, although, as all aircrew know, simulated flight is never the same as flying the actual aircraft.

Flight Test Beds
In order to test some of the new equipment to be fitted to Tornado under flight conditions, some existing aircraft were modified to carry this equipment. A Lightning was fitted with the Mauser gun, a Buccaneer with the radar and a Vulcan was modified to carry an RB 199 engine beneath its fuselage. The Vulcan installation was considerably delayed by a series of problems and did not really add very much to knowledge of the engine prior to its first flight in Tornado.

Work-up to First Flight
During the negotiating stage of the programme, the Germans had been insistent that the first flight should be made in Germany, on the grounds

Engine runs on P01 at Manching prior to first flight.

that FRG was buying more aircraft than either Britain or Italy. Sir Frederick Page reluctantly agreed to this argument, but cannily insisted that the flight should be made by a British pilot, so it came about that in early 1974, I moved to Bavaria to prepare for the occasion. I found that I was well received there and I was never made to feel that I was taking a first flight away from a German pilot, just that I was one of the team.

While the first prototype, P01, was being completed in the hangar at Manching, the aircrew busied themselves with operating the various ground systems test rigs at Ottobrun, the MBB factory, talking to the systems designers and attending the innumerable meetings that a multi-national programme of this sort seems to generate. The usual routine for testing engines on an aircraft was that the engine company engineers would do all the long-winded running-in tests, but Neils Meister, the MBB project pilot, and I decided that we would do all of the ground engine running ourselves, which would get us thoroughly at home in the cockpit and familiar with operating the systems. When P01 had its first engines fitted, we put this plan into action and spent many hours of useful work in the cockpits. We alternated between the front and rear cockpits, despite there being no controls in the rear cockpit of P01, because it was very useful to be able to talk to each other about the tests and it also helped to consolidate the already good team spirit. Taxying trials came up in due course and it was a great boost to everyone to get the aircraft moving under its own power. This also provided the opportunity to check out the telemetry system which was to be used to monitor all of the early test flying. High speed taxy trials followed, along with testing of the reverse thrust system. There was an inevitable temptation when checking the nosewheel lifting speed on the long runway at Manching to lift the aircraft clear of the ground for a short hop, but the aircraft was a political hot potato and the engines were not flight cleared so I resisted the temptation and put the nosewheel back down again.

The first flight-cleared engines arrived and were fitted to P01. With thoughts of an imminent flight, Nils Meister and I went out to do our final pre-flight engine run. When the left engine was opened up to full dry (non-reheated) power it wound up as usual to full rpm at which point the compressor exploded with an impressive noise. I returned to Warton to await further developments and Turbo-Union went back to Munich to find out what they had done wrong.

Tornado First Flight – 14 August 1974
After a pause of some four months, a pair of flight modified engines were ready for the aircraft and we went back into flight preparation mode. All went well this time, right up to the attempt to start engines for the actual flight. The Tornado engines are started from an internal auxiliary power unit. The drive from the APU to the engine gearbox contains a small, necked shaft to act as a weak link in case of gearbox seizure. This shaft had failed and there was no spare shaft at Manching. Undaunted, Herr Herrold, the aircraft crew chief, asked me to stay in the cockpit and disappeared, clutching the pieces of the minute shaft in his leather gloves. When he reappeared with a look of triumph on his face, he showed me the shaft which he had taken to the workshop and brazed together so expertly that the join barely showed. The shaft was refitted and the APU restarted; the engines then started perfectly.

Despite the rather uncertain start, the flight went perfectly from then on. Tornado was the first aircraft in Europe to be designed as a fly-by-wire machine without direct mechanical connection from the stick to the control surfaces, but from the time it left the ground it flew so beautifully that the thought of this did not occur to me. As planned, I left the aircraft in the take off configuration and climbed to 10 000 feet before cleaning up and carrying out a pre-planned series of handling tests. Aircraft handling was delightful, as anticipated - much better than the simulator - and all the aircraft systems behaved perfectly, with the possible exception

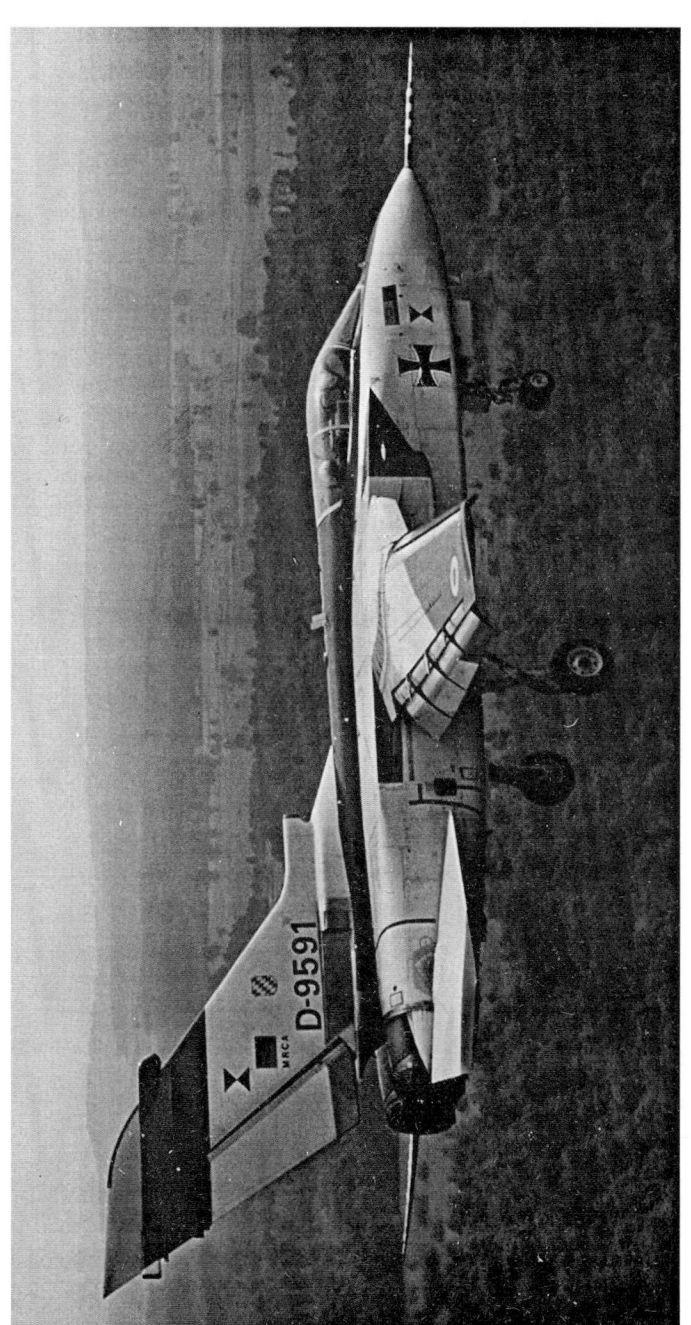
Prototype P01 on approach to Manching, August 1974.

of an occasional howl from the air conditioning system, which was easily cured after flight and never recurred. I checked the low speed handling in the landing configuration and found the aircraft to be very responsive in pitch, but nothing that worried me about the landing approach to come. I went back to the Manching airfield circuit and made a low approach and overshoot, followed by a very easily made landing. I had practised the first flight so often by this time, in simulators, and even by flying around the projected route in the Company HS125, and the actual flight went so smoothly that I did begin to wonder whether this was not yet another simulation.

Subsequent Flights on P01

The second flight was used to extend the handling envelope up to the initial limits of 3G and 300 kts. The wings were swept for the first time, with virtually no trim changes or change in handling characteristics, which showed that the aerodynamicists bad done their job well. The excellent handling found on the first flight was fully confirmed and the air conditioning noise experienced on that flight had been cured. After landing there were no faults to be reported.

The initial flight test programme had laid down that I should make the first three flights, then hand the aircraft over to the MBB pilots. Since the first two flights had gone so well, I could see no reason for not getting the German pilots in on the flying of their aircraft right away, so on Flight No 3, I sat in the back of P01 with Nils Meister at the controls and he confirmed the delightful aircraft handling. I was quite content to leave the subsequent flying of P01 to the MBB aircrews, but I was delighted to be invited to return to Manching to make Flight No 8, which was to be a demonstration of the aircraft for the benefit of the Defence Ministries and Air Staffs of the three countries, as well as introducing it to the aviation press.

To show our confidence in the aircraft, I had the aircraft parked in front of the VIP grandstand, and did away with all the usual paraphernalia of equipment and ground crew that surround most military aircraft before flight. The only person outside the aircraft was Herr Herrold, the crew chief. I started the APU on the aircraft internal battery and did a quick run through of the pre-start checks (I had previously checked everything necessary in slow time). I then started the engines, checked the controls and taxied out. It was also hoped that this demonstrated how the Tornado could operate, if necessary, from a remote base without the need for extensive back-up facilities. The flight demonstration consisted of a run through the full cleared flight envelope, showing as much manoeuvrability as possible, the full range of wing sweep, rapid roll capability, acceleration in full reheat and a short landing run using reverse thrust. From the post-flight comments, this was all well received.

Tornado P02

The second prototype, P02, was close behind P01 in construction at Warton. Dave Eagles and I operated the same routine that had been established at Manching and we did all of the engine running and ground systems testing ourselves. For the first flight, it was considered to be a valuable gesture of solidarity to invite Pietro Trevisan, the Aeritalia chief test pilot to fly in the back seat, so I had the pleasure of his company on this flight on 30th October. There had been considerable problems in setting up the flight control system on P02, so we decided to make the first flight in 'direct link'. What this meant was that the pilot control inputs would he signalled directly to the control actuators, without any computer generated inputs, in other words, without autostabilisation. The aircraft Command and Stability Augmentation System (CSAS) has three modes: full CSAS; direct link; and manual, which clutches in a mechanical connection between the control column and the all-moving tailplane. The flight was a good one in which we went around the full initially cleared flight envelope, including a short supersonic run and found that the basic aircraft without autostabilisation still flew pretty well. Full marks again to the aerodynamicists. We did have an unexplained engine problem on this flight, however. When I opened the throttles to full power before releasing the brakes, the left engine surged with an almighty bang. I throttled back and discussed the situation with a 'boffin' on the telemetry desk. They did not know what had caused the engine stall, so I rechecked full power on the left engine with no further problems. The engines looked OK from the cockpit indications and telemetry, with many more read-outs, could see nothing wrong, which caused the 'boffin' to say, 'We don't know what the problem was. It is up to you whether you go or not.' So I went!

Much later on, it was found that the early engines needed warming up at high rpm before going to full power, apparently because the internal tolerances were very tight and parts of the engine warmed up faster than other bits, causing unwanted airflow disturbances and compressor stalls.

The first flight of P02 took off before the majority of the Warton workforce had arrived for work. When I came back to the airfield, I found that word had rapidly spread that P02 was airborne and, instead of going to their offices and workshops, it appeared that everyone had come out to the airfield to watch their new aircraft. I found this a very heart warming sight, so I cheered them all up by making a couple of low level rolls down the runway before landing.

P02's primary task was to extend the clean aircraft flight envelope. All nine prototypes were allocated different tasks in order to clear the aircraft for use in their respective Services, although there was some inevitable overlap and changes of task as time went by.

P02 was fitted with 'bonkers', small explosive charges on the wings, which could be fired to excite an oscillation in the control surfaces. The damping of this oscillation could then be assessed to ensure that the aircraft was well clear of any potential flutter problems and the aircraft could then go on to make further 'bonker' tests at a higher speeds.

On one of these envelope expansion flights on P02, the engine oil temperature and oil low pressure warning lights illuminated on the right engine. I throttled that engine back and the warning lights went out. Discussion with the 'boffin' confirmed no engine problems on telemetry, so I decided to discontinue the high speed tests on that flight and revert to a secondary task, which consisted of flypasts of the control tower at the airfield with kinetheodolites recording height and speed to check cockpit instrument pressure errors. I left the right engine throttled back to idle for these tests in case of further engine oil problems. On one of these flypasts at slow speed with wheels and flaps down a seagull appeared too late for me to avoid it and it was ingested by the left engine, terminally damaging both the seagull and the engine. All the cockpit warning lights and alarms came on as I shut down the left engine and hopefully slammed the right engine throttle from idle to maximum reheat, at the same time raising the wheels and starting to bring the flaps up. The aircraft was at this time slowly sinking from its already low height down towards the ground, so I warned Dave Eagles to prepare to eject. The aircraft should have been able to climb away on one engine, but this just happened to be the first time that reheat had failed to light on selection! As a result, the reheat nozzle was fully open without reheat being lit, which caused a considerable reduction in the dry power thrust. Luckily, the engine did not like being treated like this, so it surged and the reheat nozzle closed, producing enough thrust to allow us to climb up out of the weeds and turn around for a thankful landing. On inspecting the engine with the oil problem after flight, it was found that the oil system was full of carbon. One of the engine seals which had been exposed to dynamic air pressure as the aircraft speed increased, had allowed this pressure into the engine oil system and, like a diesel engine, the oil had actually caught fire.

On a later envelope expansion flight, after rectification of the oil seal defect, a frighteningly loud noise appeared abruptly and disappeared just as quickly as I throttled back and slowed down. As there was no obvious cause for this noise, I tentatively increased speed again and the noise reappeared at the same speed. Several more attempts were made to pinpoint the source of this very loud noise when Ray Woollett, Warton's chief navigator, said from the rear seat, 'I've got it. As we accelerate, I can see the rubber canopy seal stretching higher and higher until at the point where the noise starts, it becomes invisible.' After flight the canopy seal was trimmed back and the noise did not recur.

It is of interest that prior to Tornado flying, some noise experts from Farnborough had predicted that the cockpit would be very noisy and that this noise would become limiting at high speeds. In fact, the cockpit environment was very pleasant and comfortable, both for temperature and lack of excessive noise. The Farnborough team asked if they could measure the cockpit noise levels and wired up the cockpit and ourselves with microphones and recorders to be turned on at appropriate speeds. Nothing more was heard of these tests and when I made enquiries many months later I was told that the noise levels recorded were so low that Farnborough had concluded that they had a problem with their recorders.

We then turned our attention to extending the supersonic flight envelope clearance. The early flight engines were a long way short of their required thrust so supersonic acceleration was very slow and fuel was being used up very quickly. A solution was to use in-flight refuelling so the IFR probe was fitted and checked and the flight refuelling clearance was brought forward to much earlier in the programme than had been envisaged. The Royal Air Force was extremely co-operative over the use of their tanker aircraft and clearance to flight refuel was very expeditious. Tornado handles so well and is so stable a platform that flight refuelling is easier with her than with any other aircraft that I have flight refuelled with. After the initial dry contacts with the flight refuelling basket at varying speeds and altitudes, I filled up the tanks to full and set off south down the Irish Sea from the Mull of Galloway without any fuel worries. After that, it seemed that whenever we wanted to make another supersonic clearance flight, there just happened to be a tanker aircraft exercising in the Irish Sea with some fuel to spare for us.

By this time, the third prototype, P03, was flying from Warton. This was the first dual-control aircraft and was tasked with flying with heavy loads under the wings and fuselage. P02 had already cleared the wing tanks for flutter and progressive clearances were made on the whole range of external stores to be carried.

P04 flew shortly after P03, in September 1975 from Manching. This was the first aircraft with the full Tornado avionics system and was tasked with clearing the navigation, autopilot and ground mapping systems.

The first Italian prototype, P05 flew from Caselle in December 1975. Like P02, the CSAS had been troublesome to get ready for flight, so it also flew in direct link mode. By Flight No 5 the CSAS was ready for flight. Pietro Trevisan switched it on in flight for a brief check and pronounced it satisfactory. While on the landing approach at the end of the flight, it was suggested that Trevisan should switch to full CSAS again. The CSAS approach mode was the very responsive mode mentioned previously and Trevisan was using the larger stick inputs required in direct link mode. The result was a divergent pilot induced pitch oscillation. At the bottom of one of these oscillations the aircraft contacted the runway, suffering considerable damage. Happily, the pilot was unhurt, but P05 was then out of the development programme for just over two years.

P06, the third British prototype also flew in December 1975. This aircraft was fitted with two Mauser guns and the flight test instrumentation, which was fitted in the ammunition bays on other prototypes, was placed in the rear cockpit, so P06 could only be flown solo.

Airframe Modifications

Very few airframe modifications were required to be made during the development programme. In the transonic flight regime, a shock wave at the base of the fin reduced the fin effectiveness and caused a reduction in directional stability. Fitting a row of vortex generators on either side of the lower fin cured this problem.

Some buffet and increased drag were also noted at high subsonic speeds and an improved fillet between the base of the fin and the fuselage was devised by filling in this area with a foam plastic shape that could be carved to a new shape between flights. A short intensive flying programme produced the optimum profile for this fillet which was subsequently retrofitted to all aircraft.

The position of the reverse thrust buckets behind the engine tailpipes at the very aft end of the aircraft was destabilising during reverse thrust deceleration on the landing run. This sometimes called for some fast footwork on the runway and this problem became critical when P03 ran off the runway onto soft ground when landing in heavy rain and a strong crosswind. It was also reported that one of the MBB aircraft had made an inadvertent 360 degree turn on its landing run. We had heard that SAAB had had similar problems with the Viggen in reverse thrust, so we requested a visit to Linköping to discuss it with them. Dave Eagles and I flew a small team of designers over there in the company HS125 and found the Swedish design team very helpful and open in explaining their problems and solutions. The outcome for Tornado was that, in effect, the aircraft yaw damper was connected to the nosewheel steering system. Once this had been done it was possible to land the aircraft, select full reverse thrust and run straight down the runway without touching the rudder pedals at all.

Engine Problems
When manoeuvring at 0.6-0.7M at high incidence, the left engine was prone to surge with loud machine-gun-like noises and impressive sheets of flame from the tailpipe. Embarrassingly, this was just the area of flight in which we needed to be for displaying Tornado to VIPs and at air displays. After some heated discussion between the intake designers and the engine manufacturers as to whether the problem was one of intake distortion or the engine's being too sensitive to small airflow disturbances, a small fillet was fitted onto an intake lower corner and the problem was cured. Another intake problem was discovered at a later date during the supersonic envelope expansion on P02. Just as we were close to reaching the clearance of the significant figure of Mach 2, it was found to be impossible to get past 0.92M without encountering violent intake

bangs and engine stalls. This problem was put down to an unwanted shock wave generated in an intake upper corner and was cured by fitting a vortex generator in the offending corner.

On post-flight inspection after many development flights, one or more turbine blades were found to be missing, but it is interesting that the loss of these blades was never noticed by the pilots.

Weapons System Testing

Tornado prototypes P07 and P08 flew for the first time in 1976 at Manching and Warton respectively. These aircraft were fully up to date with their avionics and, since a large part of the aircraft flight envelope, both with and without external stores, had by then been cleared, the emphasis began to focus on testing the aircraft as a complete weapons system. Aircraft handling with a variety of external stores remained as good as with the clean aircraft and an intensive programme of weapon aiming and releases, gun firing, avionics and radar testing got into full swing. Automatic terrain following tests were made over northern England and Scotland. Because the emphasis for these tests was, quite rightly, on flight safety, the early terrain following flights were made in clear weather. Even so, they could be quite harrowing for the pilot because the system was configured such that, if any of the in-built checking system detected an anomaly, an automatic pull-up was triggered. The terrain following system was designed to extremely tight tolerances, which detected many spurious errors, so on the initial flight tests the pilot had to undergo numerous unexpected sudden 3G pull-ups. I happily left this testing to our avionics specialist, John Cockburn.

Pre-series Aircraft

Production of the prototypes was completed by the first flight of P09 in Italy in February 1977. Later the same day, P11, the first of six pre-series aircraft also flew. These aircraft were used to back-up the development programme and subsequently to go either to the respective Service test flying units for evaluation, or direct to the Services after conversion to full production standard.

Further Development Flying

Tornado development flying continued at a high rate through 1977 and 1978 with so many aircraft in the programme. A number of Service VIPs were introduced to Tornado, and were all suitably impressed. A Canadian

P09, the second of two Italian prototypes.

Air Force team also came to Warton to evaluate the aircraft, although nothing was heard subsequently from Canada.

Tornado P02 was fitted with an anti-spin parachute and an emergency power unit (EPU) and commenced a series of handling tests at high incidence preparatory to full spinning trials. P02 recommenced high speed flight envelope tests in early 1979 and this time it had no problems in reaching the Mach 2 test point. After hitting Mach 2 in March 1979, I dived the aircraft, holding the Mach number constant, aiming for a flutter check at the corner point of M=2 and 800 kts IAS. P02 had never been fitted with a head-up display, so I was using the standard head-down cockpit flight instruments. Despite steepening the dive considerably, I was unable to get the airspeed indicator to go far past about 780 kts when 'boffin' said, with some alarm in his voice, 'Slow down! You are going too fast!' It turned out that the airspeed indicator had a stop at 800 kts, but this was a compressible stop acting from about 775 kts. The ground telemetry indications had gone off the clock also and it was estimated that the actual IAS had been between 820 and 830 kts.

Later that month I flew P15 to check the 1.8M/800 kt point and, using the head-up display digital readout, I was proudly holding what I thought was a superbly accurate 800 kts, when I was once again told that I was

The ill-fated P08 in full afterburner

going too fast. The head-up display specification calls for it to read up to 800 knots and that is what it does - and no more. Tragically, P08 and its crew were lost in an accident in June 1979 and similarly P04 and its crew were lost in an accident in Germany in May 1980. Inevitably, these losses caused some delays to the test programme, but the test aircraft were designed to be able to carry out multiple tasks, so the disruption was minimised.

Spinning Trials

Full spinning trials started with P02 in January 1980. Modern military aircraft do not possess a conventional stall, they usually reach an angle of incidence where directional control is lost and the aircraft yaws into a fully developed spin. Because it was expected that the engines would not be able to cope with air coming into the intakes at up to 90 degrees from straight ahead, a hydrazine emergency power unit was fitted to P02 and connected to the gearboxes supplying hydraulic and electrical power to the aircraft. This EPU was switched on just before each individual spin test.

Tests were made at all wing sweep positions and in every case it was found that the aircraft did depart into a fully developed spin, but also that the engines would be forced into a silent stall and would overheat if not shut down immediately. The spin was quite oscillatory and it was an interesting exercise for the pilot to evaluate what was happening in the spin, watch the engine temperatures and shut the engines down when necessary, apply spin recovery action, check that the spin was fully recovered, relight the engines, shut down the EPU and then climb back up to 40 000 feet for the next test.

The first spin tests were made from standard straight slowdowns, but later in the trials we pulled the aircraft to high angles of incidence in dynamic tests from higher airspeeds. In one of these tests I had pulled full back stick and reached an angle of incidence of 45 degrees when 'boffin' told me to recover because the EPU had failed. My cockpit indications were all normal, but it was found after flight that the drive shaft connecting the EPU to the gearbox had failed. Happily, this was one occasion in which the aircraft did *not* yaw off into a spin.

Naturally we did not recommend that Service aircraft should be cleared for spinning.

Production Aircraft.
The first British production Tornado, BT001, made its first flight in July 1979 and was subsequently taken to Boscombe Down for weapons trials. BT002 flew in December 1979 and on 1st July 1979 I was delighted to take the aircraft, with Ollie Heath in the rear seat, on its delivery flight to the TTTE at Cottesmore to be handed over to the Services. We believed that we were giving the air forces an excellent product, which would serve them well.

INTO SERVICE - TRAINING & OPERATIONS
Air Vice-Marshal R P O'Brien

Bob O'Brien flew Canberras and Buccaneers in the reconnaissance and strike/attack roles in RAF Germany before moving on to the Tornado in 1980. Having converted to the aircraft with MBB in Munich he became Chief Instructor at the Tri-national Tornado Training Establishment when it formed in 1981, subsequently commanding RAF Marham in 1983-85 during the build up and operational declaration of the UK Tornado Force. Following tours at MOD in the Air Offensive Directorate and other Headquarters he retired in 1998.

My intention this afternoon is to pick up the Tornado story from the point at which it entered service. I will look at the operational capability of the early GR1s, how they were initially deployed and how they met the operational need. I also want to cover the training dimension, because this was an integral part of getting the aircraft into service and reflects the different flying philosophies and requirements of the four Services involved. I should point out at this stage that the fourth Service is the German Naval Air Arm, which eventually operated two wings of Tornados, in addition to the air forces of the UK, Germany and Italy.

TRAINING

Tri-National Plans

Given the multi-national development and procurement programme for Tornado, it was a natural extension of the process for the three MODs to consider aircrew training on a joint basis. As with some of the early national aspirations for the range and capability of the aircraft, not all the training aims were achieved. Nevertheless, a Tri-National Tornado Training Establishment (TTTE) was formed and joint conversion training took place very successfully for some nineteen years, until the establishment was closed in 1999 and the three nations elected to go their separate ways.

The training story started in June 1972, some two years before the flight of the first Tornado prototype, when the Joint Operational Training Study Committee (JOTSC) met to discuss the feasibility of carrying out,

'Some or all MRCA training on a co-operative basis'. The JOTSC was a wing commander/lieutenant colonel-level Air Staff group representing the three nations, which in due course was to become a sub-committee of the Tornado Steering Committee (TSC), when it formed in 1976. The TSC operated at colonel/one-star-level with the principal UK representative being Director Training (Flying) RAF. The TSC rotated its chairmanship between the nations and was very much the driving force behind the setting up and running of TTTE. This committee structure, which also included Engineering, Personnel and Finance sub-groups, was arguably bureaucratic and certainly slowed decision making. However, given the significant financial commitment involved in joint training, and the occasional weakening of resolve along the line shown by individual nations, it served to ensure that all concerns were addressed and the politically important goal of joint training was achieved. In March 1975 the JOTSC recommended Tri-National Training at two levels: a Joint Operational Conversion Unit at RAF Cottesmore and a Joint Weapons Conversion Unit at the Italian Air Force base at Decimomannu on Sardinia.

The arguments that led to the proposal for a Joint OCU at RAF Cottesmore were fairly predictable, given the national positions on procurement of the aircraft. The Italians were the junior partners in terms of airframes ordered and not in a position to press for the use of an Italian base. The Germans, by contrast, could probably have made a base available; however, much of their training was conducted in the United States and their MOD was already coming under considerable pressure over low flying complaints from the many NATO aircraft already based on their soil. The German commitment to joint training was also less firm during this period. This put the UK, who were very keen to maintain the RAF's tradition of being closely involved in its own training, in a strong position.

RAF Cottesmore presented an ideal location. It was large, reasonably modern and unoccupied, having only recently been put on Care and Maintenance as a result of the 1975 Defence Review. The recommendation to form a joint OCU at Cottesmore was therefore endorsed by the national MODs and the arrangement formalised in a Memorandum of Understanding signed in May 1979. Under the proposal, refurbishment costs were to be strictly controlled and existing facilities used wherever possible. A notable exception was the completely new approach to be taken to engine maintenance, with the conversion of a complete aircraft hangar to an on-base Engine Repair Factory. The modular design of the RB 199 engine allowed on-base replacement of major components, such as compressors and turbines with engines effectively rebuilt *in situ*. It was claimed that this process, albeit expensive in terms of Service manpower, would greatly speed up repair turn round times. On base Engine Repair Factories were, I believe, a success and subsequently adopted on all RAF Tornado main operating bases. The provision of a large aircraft servicing platform, capable of operating up to twenty-eight Tornados, was also considered essential to handle the large number of aircraft needed each day to achieve the TTTE flying task.

The proposal to conduct joint weapons training was, however, far more problematic and eventually foundered. The Italian suggestion, to base a Weapons Conversion Unit at Decimomannu, was predicated on expanding the capacity of the nearby NATO Range at Capo Frasca.. The details of the proposals, which were put to the JOTSC were 'novel' in concept, to say the least. The Italians suggested dividing the range into two halves so that both target complexes could be used simultaneously. The left range would be used on a left-hand pattern and the right range on a right-hand pattern with, *in the ideal case*, some 7000 feet laterally between aircraft attacking on parallel tracks. Up to four aircraft would be simultaneously allowed in each half, which would have a separate controller and RT frequency. A master controller would be in overall charge! After some eight hours of discussion within the JOTSC and a visit to the range, it became clear that the proposal did not enjoy universal support. Indeed, the recorded national reactions to the proposals give an illuminating insight into the different attitudes of the air forces concerned. The Italians, as originators of the proposal, considered it acceptable. The UK representative rejected it on the grounds of both safety and effectiveness. He pointed out that aircraft could be on head-on flightpaths on the base leg of opposing ranges at closing speeds of up to 900kts, on different frequencies, and rolling in belly-up to the other aircraft whilst trying to acquire the target. This, he argued, was hardly a sensible environment for a student crew. The German delegate shared the UK's concern, but decided to refer the matter to higher authority. In the end each nation decided to conduct its own weapons training, which in the case of the RAF took place at the Tornado Weapons Conversion Unit at RAF Honington. This decision, which was undoubtedly seen as disappointing at the time, was probably a blessing in disguise. Had combined weapons training gone ahead it would have been at a considerable cost, not only in finding an acceptable range and base, but also in the significant compromises that would have been needed in putting together a training course for the diverse weapons and electronic warfare systems which each nation intended to use on Tornado.

Tornado Training

Steady progress was, however, made towards setting up the Joint OCU. In early in 1978 a course design team was formed under the leadership of an RAF wing commander to create a syllabus to meet the objectives of the three air forces and the German Navy. Their task immediately revealed the very different operational background and requirements of the air arms concerned. Whilst both the Germans and Italians had operated in the strike and attack roles, they were single-seat orientated, with a long history of flying the F-104, and before that the F-84. The British, by contrast, had flown predominantly two-seat strike and attack aircraft dating back through the Buccaneer, Phantom and Canberra. As a consequence, the Italians had no experienced fast jet navigators, and within the German air arms experience was limited to those who had flown in the small force of F-4 Phantoms in the attack and recce roles. The need to ensure correct crew co-operation and workload was, of course, fundamental to the operation of Tornado, where control of most of the nav/attack system (and therefore the success of the mission) lay in the rear seat. Despite the fact that the Germans had insisted on fitting a radar repeater in the front seat of their aircraft, to allow greater pilot involvement, the RAF philosophy of two-seat operations and shared crew workload was quickly accepted as the norm. Whilst one should not seek to overplay the importance of the RAF lead in this area, I believe that effective crew co-operation, as demonstrated by some extremely capable RAF navigators, was one of the major contributions that our Service flying syllabus, covering transition, formation, navigation, terrain following and simulated weapon attacks by day and night was agreed. It comprised four weeks of ground school and synthetic training, followed by a nine-week flying phase and required some 35 hours for pilots and 28 hours for navigators.

The first aircraft (a British trainer, B01) was delivered to Cottesmore on 1 June 1980 and by the official opening of TTTE on 29 January 1981,

First air-to-air picture of a tri-national formation, 26 May 1982. The crews were B55 – Wg Cdr O'Brien & Sqn Ldr Morris; G73 – Maj Jung & Flt Lt Heath and I40 – Lt Col Cariati & Hptm Guetter.

there were some fourteen aircraft on strength. The full establishment of forty-eight Tornados (twenty-two German, nineteen British and seven Italian) was achieved in August 1982. In addition to the radarscope in the front seat of the German aircraft, there were other national variations. All the UK aircraft, for example had a fin fuel tank, reflecting the UK's concern about range. This was to prove very useful at TTTE, as external fuel tanks were not carried. Whilst the IFF, radio and Radar Warning Receivers were also different in each nation's aircraft, they presented no difficulty to the aircrew, although some were rather more 'user friendly' than others. Perhaps understandably, an attempt by the RAF at TTTE to point out the superior handling qualities of both the German IFF and radios was not well received by higher authority in MOD(UK). Aircrew conversion to Tornado proved to be relatively straightforward. Although the first Cottesmore-based simulator was not available until the Spring of 1982, some fifteen months after training commenced, the aircraft's excellent handling qualities and sophisticated nav/attack system made it comparatively easy to fly and operate at low level. Training of first tourists started with No 23 Course in August 1982 and presented few problems; indeed there were no student failures on the main course at all during the first two years, although one pilot failed to achieve an instructor category. The main difficulty during the early days at TTTE stemmed from the slow arrival of Release To Service clearances and shortages of some critical spares. As a result of some extremely hard work by the engineers, and the occasional resort to robbing to provide spares, monthly flying hour targets were generally met. In September 1981 the unit exceeded 500 hrs for the first time and by March 1982, when the requirement was just over 650 hrs, the unit actually flew some 970 hrs, which helped to make up for earlier poor winter weather. Although the aircraft could be navigated extremely accurately from the outset, Terrain Following (TF) was limited to the manual backup system with automatic TF not cleared for some eighteen months.

Conversion to flying a swing-wing aircraft posed few problems, thanks to the excellent fly-by-wire control system. However, as the aircraft cannot be landed by the instructor from the rear seat with the wings swept fully aft, (the approach speed is in the order of 200kts with a very high angle of attack), significant effort was put into training students early in the course for this unlikely, but demanding, event. Fortunately, this training paid off when in the second month of flying at Cottesmore an aircraft was safely landed in this configuration, an occurrence which has proved to be extremely rare during Tornado's subsequent service.

Another feature of the aircraft that exercised minds at TTTE during the early days was the working of the undercarriage and weight-on-wheels microswitches. The problem lay in the practice amongst certain ex-F-104 pilots of selecting the undercarriage up when almost airborne and relying on the microswitches to stop retraction until the aircraft was safely clear of the ground. Whilst this might have worked on the F-104, and prevented overstressing the undercarriage as the aircraft accelerated extremely quickly, it was not the case on Tornado which would sink back onto the runway. Several such incidents, which resulted in Cat 3 or 4 damage, occurred during the early years. One unlucky airframe, I-40, which was the first Italian aircraft to arrive at Cottesmore, took some thirty months to repair following such an incident. A photograph taken inside the cockpit as the aircraft was removed from the runway showed the undercarriage selector firmly in the 'UP' position.

On the personnel side relationships between the aircrew of the three nations at Cottesmore were extremely harmonious from the outset and the unit quickly evolved its own unique character and *esprit de corps*. A potential source of friction did emerge during the Falklands War in 1982, when some of the Italians who had Argentinean relatives, (including one Argentinean wife) expressed concern about the UK's military action. Fortunately, it was quickly over. The command structure by which an RAF Station Commander shared responsibility with a Senior National Representative from the German and Italian Air Forces, worked well. Command of the Joint OCU rotated at wing commander level between the nations and within each flying squadron there was a completely integrated instructor cadre.

Some compromises were, however, necessary in the way TTTE operated. As the Germans and Italians were being instructed in a language that was not their own, the pace was somewhat slower than one would have found in an RAF OCU. However, the quality of the product was none the worse for that, allowing some of the weaker students to progress more slowly. By the end of the first four years of training only two individuals had failed subsequently to graduate from their national weapons training units. Some administrative procedures, such as the investigation of aircraft incidents and accidents, were modified and a Tornado Combined Safety Investigation (TCSI) adopted. The TCSI was charged with investigating the facts only, leaving considerations of blame for subsequent national legal procedures; a foretaste of the changes that have since taken place in RAF Boards of Inquiry concerning findings of negligence.

Costs at TTTE were shared roughly on a 40:40:20 ratio between the UK, Germany and Italy respectively, with fine tuning done at the end of each accounting period on the actual number of aircrew training hours flown. By the time the TTTE closed in March 1999 it had trained some 4500 aircrew and amassed over 162 000 flying hours, of which the Germans had flown 47.5 %, the UK 40.8% and the Italians 11.7%. During the nineteen years of training just three aircraft were lost; two of which were in low level mid-air collisions and the third involved an inexperienced student during a simulated weapons attack in difficult weather.

OPERATIONS

RAF Frontline

The first task of TTTE had been to complete the instructor cadre, initially providing Instructor Pilots and Navigators for Cottesmore and subsequently for the national weapons conversion units at RAF Honington and GAF Jever. By August 1981 the Commanding Officers of both WCU's had graduated and with TTTE now able to train seven crews per main course, both units rapidly achieved their establishments. The RAF Tornado Weapons Conversion Unit (TWCU) officially opened on 8 January 1982, some twelve months after the TTTE. By May 1982 Cottesmore was able to train ten crews per course and the build up of the operational squadrons was able to begin. June 1982 was a significant milestone in the re-equipment programme, as the Royal Air Force formally entered the Tornado era with the formation of the first UK operational squadron, No 9 Sqn at Honington. This was followed by Nos 617 and 27 Sqns at Marham in October 1982 and March 1983 respectively. Each squadron had an establishment of twelve GR1s, (of which one was a dual-control trainer for check flights and instrument training) and fifteen crews, giving an aircraft aircrew ratio of 1.3:1.

The UK-based squadrons were all earmarked for declaration to NATO as dual capable in the fighter-bomber strike/attack roles and integrated into the Central Region's strike and attack plans. Squadron work up priority was firmly directed towards the strike role and meeting national commitments made to support SACEUR's nuclear Launch Sequence Plan (LSP). Each unit was allowed twelve months from formation to achieve combat ready status, and had to pass a Tactical Evaluation before being declared in the strike role. This presented a significant challenge in the support areas, as neither Honington nor Marham had operated strike aircraft, with the attendant command and control and security procedures, for many years. Furthermore, Marham's Supplementary Storage Area had to be refurbished to receive the WE177 weapon and a myriad of engineering and safety procedures introduced to meet the stringent criteria for handling nuclear weapons. Each of the squadrons occupied a newly built Hardened Aircraft Shelter (HAS) site with the latest standard of MK3 HAS, which could shelter two Tornados, although only one aircraft could be started inside. Aircrew and groundcrew bunkers were provided which gave a large measure of physical and NBC protection, although, unlike the RAF Germany stations, neither Honington nor Marham initially had a hardened station Operations Centre. The UK-based Tornado nuclear strike assets were therefore controlled from 1940s style operations rooms for the first two years.

In RAF Germany the Buccaneer wing at Laarbruch was the first to re-equip, with No 15 Sqn forming in September 1983 followed by No 16 Sqn in March 1984. The third Laarbruch squadron, No 20 Sqn, formed in June 1984. At Brüggen the Jaguar Wing followed quickly thereafter, with No 31 Sqn forming in September 1984, No 17 Sqn in March 1985 and No 14 Sqn in May of that year. Finally, No 9 Sqn, which had been the first UK-based squadron to form at Honington in 1982, moved to Brüggen in October1986 to bring the wing up to its full strength of four squadrons. Nuclear QRA was held by Tornados at Laarbruch and Brüggen but not by the squadrons in the UK. By the end of 1986 the re-equipment programme was complete, with seven squadrons in RAF Germany and two at Marham. The total Royal Air Force ORBAT was therefore nine squadrons of GR1s, comprising some 108 aircraft, operationally declared in the strike and attack roles. The final phase of the Tornado GR1s entry to service took place in 1989 and 1990 when No 2 Sqn formed at Laarbruch and No 13 Sqn at Honington, both equipped with the GR1A reconnaissance variant of the aircraft.

Operational Capability
In assessing the extent to which the introduction of the Tornado GR1 increased the RAF's operational capability, it is important to examine these improvements against the threats and requirements of the 1980s. The most obvious and fundamental improvement was that Tornado provided, for the first time, a genuine and credible blind strike/attack capability. The aircraft had the necessary systems to penetrate likely enemy defences and deliver an effective suite of weapons with considerable accuracy, at low level, at night and in all weathers. Whilst previous aircraft, such as the Buccaneer, Phantom and Jaguar, had claimed a limited ability to operate in this environment, the results were unpredictable and their survival and effectiveness questionable, given the heights at which they would have been forced to fly and their inferior navigation and weapons delivery systems. The Tornado's nav/attack system represented a quantum jump in terms of accuracy and ease of use. Based around an inertial navigation system with Kalman filtering it would typically produce drift rates of around one nautical mile per hour. However, when updated by fixes from the ground mapping radar the overall system error could easily be maintained at around 0·2 nautical miles or less.

By feeding this level of accuracy into the pilot's moving map display very precise en route navigation could be achieved, which allowed the crew to concentrate on flying visually at around 200 ft during the penetration phase. If the tactical situation required it, the aircraft could operated down to 100ft, although the crew workload increased considerably at such heights. The automatic terrain following system, which was based on a separate terrain following radar (TFR) linked to the autopilot, was very effective and combat-ready crews had no difficulty in operating at night or in poor weather down to 200 feet above ground level. The TF system which was based on a Texas Instruments radar was proven and mature, with a number of safety features and a good serviceability record. The crew could monitor its performance, which enhanced safety, although nuisance warnings, resulting in a spurious pull-up command, would occasionally happen. An impressive testament to the integrity of the TFR system is that, throughout the aircraft's service life, it has enjoyed a 100% safety record and, despite some demanding usage, no Tornado has ever been lost as a result of a TFR malfunction. In addition to the strike role, where aircraft operated as singletons, TFR was possible on attack missions where concentration of force over a target was often a requirement. By means of the parallel track TFR technique formations of up to four aircraft could penetrate whilst maintaining formation integrity to conduct a visual or blind attack.

Whether flying visually or using TFR a properly managed nav/attack system gave Tornado crews a very high level of navigational accuracy, which had the added advantage of allowing the crew to evade airborne and ground based threats should they arise whilst progressing to the target. Electronic protection was provided by a combination of the Radar Warning Receiver, ECM and chaff and flare pods. The Skyshadow Mk1 ECM pod provided active countermeasures against the current generation of SAM and radar-laid gun threats, and together with the BOZ chaff and flare dispenser, was carried as a standard fit on an outboard pylon on all sorties. During the weapons delivery phase, blind attacks could be carried out using the radar in either a direct or offset mode to provide accurate release cues for both laydown and lofted weapons. Alternatively, the pilot could take control if he saw the target and continue with a visual attack assisted, if necessary, by laser ranging.

There are, of course, two other considerations in the capability equation; notably range and weapon delivery. As regards range, there is no hiding the fact that in the GR1 we are dealing with a tactical aircraft with radii of action of under 400 nmls in the lo-lo context and around 500 nmls hi-lo-hi. Both cases assume a representative war load of four 1000lb bombs and full external defensive aids. This clearly compares unfavourably with claims for the TSR2 of around 1000 nmls lo-lo, or even the Canberra which had a 600 nmls radius under similar conditions. Furthermore, 400 nmls is a best figure, based on maximum use of external tanks and carrying centre line weapons in the strike or attack roles role. In other weapons fits, such as carrying two JP233s, the range reduces to around 280 nmls lo-lo.

As to the weapons themselves, there is no question that Tornado was well equipped to meet the damage requirements and accuracy expected in the mid 1980s. In the strike role all variants of WE177 could be carried and delivered in air- or ground-burst modes well within the ACE Force Standard. In the attack role the GR1 was initially declared using the earlier generation BL755 cluster bomb, as well as the 1000lb bomb in the ballistic or retard modes and the 23mm Mauser cannon. Whilst the BL755 had acknowledged limitations in terms of pattern spread on the ground, the 1000lb bomb was considered highly effective, particularly when the newly-developed multi-function bomb fuse became available. As a foretaste of things to come, a very limited 'smart delivery' capability for the 1000lb bomb, using American laser designation equipment on an accompanying Buccaneer, was also developed by one of the RAF Germany squadrons in the late 1980s. The profile, which was particularly demanding, involved the release and guidance of the weapons from low level against some very high value targets. A further weapon, which I have mentioned already, and which was designed specifically for Tornado, became available within a few years. This was the JP233 airfield denial and runway cratering munition that had been procured specifically to meet the Offensive Counter Air need against Warsaw Pact airfields. Although JP233 required a relatively vulnerable straight and level pass over the target whilst the sub-munitions were ejected to achieve maximum effect, it represented a custom built solution against one of the major threats that faced the Central Region. Hitherto runways could not be successfully attacked from low level so the JP233-equipped Tornado represented a significant increase in capability.

Any assessment as to how effective the GR1 force would have been in meeting the threat facing the Central Region during the latter years of the Cold War can only be conjecture. However, there are a number of factors in its favour. First, the numbers involved. With some 108 strike/attack and twenty-four recce aircraft declared sufficient aircraft were available to provide significant force packages. Secondly, as a weapons system, the aircraft was well equipped to meet the threats of the day. The airframe was specifically designed for the low level environment, with excellent stability and flight characteristics which allowed the GR1 to penetrate and deliver effective weapons in all terrain and all weather conditions. It was also well equipped to defend itself with both active and passive electronic warfare systems. Its range was arguably limited but, with external fuel tanks, the Tornado could reach a large proportion of the required Central Region targets. Performance standards of both the aircrew and groundcrew within the squadrons were thoroughly and relentlessly tested by both the UKAIR and Central Region TACEVAL teams. Such evaluations, which were stringent, assessed every aspect of a Tornado unit's ability to meet its war role from aircraft serviceability and spares holdings to aircrew training records, target study and weapons knowledge. The Tornado results were impressive with most units achieving a One, or 'Excellent', rating on their initial and subsequent strike evaluations. In the attack role the ratings were normally as good, although occasionally weapon holding limitations reduced the scores. Experience on exercises such as RED FLAG and GREEN FLAG (with its enhanced electronic warfare scenarios) against state-of-the-art NATO defence units, were also an excellent indicator of the high level of success the Tornado could expect in penetrating and releasing weapons against Central Region targets.

Finally, the aircraft was also able to prove itself in the competition arena, by sweeping the board on two successive years in the USAF's Strategic Air Command Bombing Competition. In both 1984 and 1985 crews from Nos 617 and 27 Sqns at Marham took a number of major prizes in this prestigious competition, although they were required to fly a number of attacks at medium level, for which the weapons system was not optimised, and all sorties required air-to-air refuelling to give the aircraft the necessary range. In conclusion, the Tornado GR1 that entered operational service in 1982 and continued to evolve throughout that decade, was well suited to the Central Region strike/attack and recce task. Had the Cold War turned hot it would, I believe, have acquitted itself very well. It is perhaps ironic therefore that the first shots fired in anger come from the use of Tornado in the quite different scenario of the Gulf War, which, whilst not for discussion today, is the next part of the Tornado story.

Tornado GR 1, ZD851, at Muharraq in 1992.

CONCLUSIONS : INDUSTRY
John Wragg

John Wragg graduated from King's College, London with First Class Honours in mechanical engineering and, following National Service in the Army, he worked in Bath before joining the Bristol Aeroplane Company's Engine Division in 1952. He became Chief Development Engineer in 1970, General Manager of the Experimental Department in 1976 and General Manager of the Bristol site in 1977. In 1984 he was elected to the Board of Rolls-Royce and appointed Director of Corporate Engineering. He was Director Military Engines in Bristol when he finally retired in 1989. Since then he has remained active as a Visiting Professor at Bristol University where he was awarded an Honorary Doctorate in Engineering.

I will speak first of some of the significant aspects of importance to industry which have emerged from the Tornado programme, and then illustrate how Rolls-Royce, stimulated by the Tornado programme, has introduced new philosophies to achieve the requirements of its customers at affordable costs.

So, the achievements and disappointments of the Tornado programme as they affected the engine:

1. A clear definition of the customer's initial requirements was available; but the enhancements inevitably needed in the longer term were studiously ignored. As a result, performance improvements, although demonstrated (largely at Company expense), were not built upon by the customer early enough.
2. Technical boundaries between companies, where joint understandings were required, were given insufficient attention by the customer, who acted as a lawyer, rather than a catalyst.
3. The competition by which the engine was chosen would be conducted today on a basis of demonstrated evidence and not on academic papers - which were really no more that a translation of the notorious 'back of the menu card' promises.
4. Exchange of 'best practice' between partner companies did take

place, although, in relation to the product, they were mostly one way. On the other hand, the UK did receive some very useful and constructive advice on how to solve the difficult Industrial Relations problems that were dogging the programmes at that time; management and employees both learned much and the lessons were widely applied. Care was taken by all companies to prevent the transfer of 'crown jewels' at the research stage; it is of course in this early phase that competitive advantage can be lost.

5. The massive Tornado programme offered little encouragement to the partner companies to reduce costs; those companies with large programmes for commercial applications did, of course, reduce factory costs but further work on this subject is required if partnership programmes are ever to be fully competitive.

6. A broad pattern for future European collaboration by industry was tentatively set up, although not provided with the necessary quality of support. It has, however, only been a timid stepping stone to the final solution of international take-overs and mergers.

So what specific lessons can we draw from the Tornado enterprise?

Perhaps the most important one was that building on the outcome of collaboration on one project does not mean, on its own, that there is a divine right to be involved in the next one. Continuing to be an attractive partner depends, as all business depends, upon the continuation of being a relevant competitor. The management, or shareholders, who see a satisfaction in the profitability of a secure share in a massive programme, have to realise that this will only continue in the future if there is a real threat that the individual company can conceive and develop the next product better on its own than with the other partners.

And this, of course, is the message that Gordon Lewis has been preaching in his continuing advocacy of timely research and demonstration programmes. It is essential that the customer's changing demands be minimised so that their impact does not disrupt the engine development programme. And, of course, the outcome of these programmes must not be disregarded because of political or emotional dogma.

What lessons can we learn from having government as the customer?

It is clear that politicians do not have a wish to acquire any knowledge of the scientific background of industry; neither do they provide direct access to those in industry who could present the engineering imperatives for government action.

Many of those who are prepared to take a more active interest are relative juniors who cannot compete with Boards of companies who are often more concerned with the success of the next few years, and not the long term needs of the customer.

So a way still needs to be found to by-pass any intellectual baggage in the Civil Service which automatically discards all that it cannot understand, and therefore fails to present the options to ministers correctly.

And finally, a few examples of the key challenges that face industry, in general, today and which have been highlighted by the Tornado programme. These four points sum up what I have been talking about and constitute sound advice to any manufacturing company.

1. IF RESEARCH IS ONLY BEGUN WHEN A PRODUCT DEVELOPMENT PROGRAMME IS LAUNCHED THEN IT IS ALREADY TOO LATE.

2. SHAREHOLDERS AND GOVERNMENT MUST SUPPORT A CONTINUING RESEARCH AND DEVELOPMENT PROGRAMME..

3. PRODUCTS MUST BE COMPETITIVE IN BOTH PRICE AND PERFORMANCE.

4. ALL PRODUCT COSTS MUST BE IDENTIFIED AND MINIMISED IN THE INITIAL DESIGN.

CONCLUSIONS : PROCUREMENT ORGANISATION
Dr William Stewart

In 1964-65, the incoming Labour government was faced with military procurement expenditure increasing rapidly on a number of projects at the same time, exacerbated by poor forecasting of programme timescales and cost estimates and fractured project management arrangements. The reaction to the procurement budget was the cancellation of major projects and an attempt to find economies in collaboration. In January 1965, the Project Time and Cost Analysis Section was set up to provide much more detailed statistical experience of previous projects to the government and industry/government working parties. Programme management was reorganised and Project Directors given integrated technical, programme and financial responsibilities.

We had some three years of Anglo-French collaboration. This was only partially applicable. The French had an industrial capability and technology level similar to that of the UK and also similar government procurement structures. The consortium countries had much less capability in almost all areas. They would require substantial support and 'education' from the UK. We were in a new collaborative project management environment.

By the time the MRCA discussions started in 1968, government procurement management was in a much stronger position to cope with the situation, government/industry relationships had been improved and military procurement had moved into the Ministry of Technology. The close association of military and civil activities and closer association with industry in the Ministry of Technology and the strong governmental support for this Department had an important influence on MRCA. The most obvious was the support for Rolls-Royce, who were in difficulties at the time, since failure to continue in the advanced military engine field would have been disastrous. The Ministry was also concerned to maintain technical advances in the fields of equipment and avionics.

Some major decisions on how the programme would be managed had to be taken quickly. International industrial and governmental organisations were to be collocated in Munich. This was somewhat controversial but there was little that the UK could do about it at the time. With this decision, substantive industrial and governmental teams had to be set up rapidly. The provision of high quality UK staff in both sectors, their collocation, backed up by home-based staffs for the working groups and the support of our R&D establishments, ensured that the international management arrangements were made to work. There was inevitably delay in the early stages, often to the frustration of the industrial partners. However, it had to be recognised that some of the countries had not been involved in the development of an advanced combat aircraft. Conflicts over the aspirations of countries, the extent of their participation, the capability of the aircraft and the level of finance they were prepared to commit could not be avoided and took time to resolve. Much effort was devoted to trying to retain as many countries as possible in the programme. However, Belgium, Canada, and later the Dutch, decided to leave the programme. With some further concessions to Italy, the three-countries programme was agreed and more rapid progress became possible. Design and construction of the prototypes progressed well. But there was then some delay in first flight due to engine problems. Late delivery of some equipment also caused problems. Nevertheless, considering the complexity of the project, the lack of experience in the other countries and the new management agencies that had to be generated, the overall results could be regarded as successful. There was some increase in development costs but some of this was on modifications to assist in production. The consequent reduction in production cost resulted in the combined development/production programme being within 1% of the original estimate, excluding the special ADV development costs.

When it came to the next major project, Eurofighter, Spain joined Germany, Italy and the UK. The economies and successes of the international industrial/governmental complex that had already been established in Munich were such that it was almost axiomatic that the international management organisation for Eurofighter would be collocated alongside that of Tornado in Munich.

CONCLUSIONS : AN RAF VIEWPOINT
Air Vice-Marshal R P O'Brien

In providing a Royal Air Force view on the conclusions to be drawn about the birth of Tornado I believe I can do no better than to draw on the opening words of our chairman for the day, Air Chf Mshl Sir Anthony Skingsley, who, as you will recall, was CinC RAF Germany from 1987 to 1989. Sir Anthony, who had some seven operational Tornado squadrons under command, summed it up succinctly when he said that his aircrew loved flying and operating the Tornado. It is a view which I certainly endorse and one which I am sure is shared by all those at the sharp end, who were connected with this highly successful aircraft.

The reason is quite simple. For the first time in my experience of three tours in RAF Germany, we had in Tornado a weapons system that could actually do all that was asked of it and fully meet its operational declaration, by day or night. When you think about the reality of going to war in an aircraft and you are holding QRA on a 24 hour basis, it is immensely encouraging to know that the aircraft you are flying was designed and custom built for the job. Such was the case with the SACEUR-assigned GR1s operating in the low level role. By comparison with earlier generation recce and strike/attack aircraft, Tornado represented a quantum leap in capability, because it could genuinely operate in all weather by day or night and achieve penetration and weapons delivery whilst maintaining a high degree of self defence. The value of a credible low level, all weather capability cannot, to my mind, be overstated.

Whilst each of Tornado's predecessors had virtues of their own and must be compared against the threats of the day, they had a number of shortcomings when used at low level. The Canberra, for example, had an impressive range of some 600 nmls. However, the airframe was comparatively slow, with the straight wings providing an uncomfortable ride above about 400 knots. It had no defensive aids for use at low level and its visual navigation system, assisted by DECCA, if you were lucky with the DECCA 'line cut', called into question accurate weapon delivery in anything other than visual conditions. The Buccaneer and Phantom enjoyed far more suitable airframes. Indeed, the Buccaneer's ride at 550 knots was every bit as good as Tornado's, however neither aircraft had a truly effective nav/attack system. Neither the Phantom nor Buccaneer radars had been designed for overland use at low level and whilst some defensive aids were available, both aircraft would have been vulnerable at the heights needed to penetrate in all weather. The Jaguar certainly enjoyed an up to date nav/attack system, but it was hampered by the lack of any radar or a terrain following system. It was also a single seater, although I would not wish to enter into the single- versus two-seat argument here.

The answer to the requirement was the Tornado GR1. The aircraft admittedly had less range than the RAF had initially hoped for, but it could cover all the essential Central Region targets. Furthermore, in so doing it enjoyed a high probability of mission success operating equally well by day or by night. Indeed, most crews would probably have preferred to go to war in Tornado by night. Although compromises may have been necessary in terms of the tri-national procurement route needed to get Tornado at all, the end result was that the RAF achieved almost all that it wanted in terms of a two-seat, twin-engined, all weather low level recce and strike/attack aircraft. The only caveat that I must make is that I have considered the Tornado GR 1 exclusively in the low level role for which it was designed. The subsequent use of the aircraft at medium level during the conflicts of the post Cold War era, may present a different picture.

DISCUSSION

(Unfortunately, there were some problems with the audio tape which meant that some parts of the proceedings were not recorded. This was of particular significance in the context of the two discussion periods. What is reproduced below is a mixture of what was actually on the tape (suitably edited) and some of the missing exchanges which have been reconstructed in arrears in consultation with those involved. Ed.)

Jack Gordon. I seem to recall that, at one time, during the development phase, the Italians had a 15% workshare. How did that come about?

Bill Stewart. It was a 'giveaway'. We started with six countries which then fell to four and eventually to just three. The Italian position was particularly odd because of the way in which responsibility for the provision of finance was divided between their air force and their procurement organisation. They simply didn't have a method of dealing with defence projects in isolation in the way that we had. In effect, the Italians had a pot into which all Ministries put their money and as each new requirement emerged, they argued about which projects would be funded and who would handle them. It was this Council of Ministers that allocated funds to the Tornado's initial development when the project was competing for finance against things like a new organ for the Vatican! I won't list the other high priorities but you can, perhaps, see that within such a system much could depend on the pressure exerted by individuals. In the case of Tornado it was argued that their 11% workshare would buy Italy virtually no influence among NAMMA's Board of Directors and that, in any dispute, they would simply be overruled by the UK and Germany. In order to keep them in the programme, and to secure the Italian financial contribution, it was eventually agreed to give them 15% of the work at only 11% of the cost, the other two nations each chipping in the other 2%.

Patrick Hassell. Given the operational role of the aircraft as perceived in the late 1960s and the way that it has been used since, was any consideration ever given to the fact that the requirement might have been met by a new Buccaneer, a subsonic aircraft, rather than an aircraft with a Mach 2 capability, and if not, why not?

Sir Anthony Skingsley. I will ask others to comment, but I can assure you that a developed Buccaneer was certainly given serious consideration. Indeed the version of the Buccaneer that was on offer would have satisfied the range requirement even better than the aeroplane that we eventually got. There were two major drawbacks, however. First, the Buccaneer had no self-defence capability and, secondly, there was no scope whatsoever for extrapolating the design to produce a fighter variant.

Gp Capt Jock Heron. I would add that the dash speed of the Buccaneer was not perceived to be fast enough for either target penetration or egress with the load that we were planning to carry. I know that a Buccaneer, without wing tanks and with its weapons carried in an internal bomb bay, was a fast aeroplane, but we were looking for a 750 knot egress. I think experience in the Gulf showed that Tornados did leave their targets at such speeds, but Bob O'Brien is perhaps better qualified to speak on the performance of the aircraft during that sort of manoeuvre.

AVM Bob O'Brien. I think that the key consideration was that the Buccaneer, even in its slick wing version, lacked the potential to become a fighter. Having said that, I can tell you, as an operator, that the speeds used for ingress to the target in a Tornado were very similar to those of the Buccaneer and, dare I say it, in some configurations actually slighter slower. Nevertheless you could jettison the stores and come home very fast indeed and I suspect that if we had ever had to go to war, and fortunately I never did, that is what would have counted most.

Skingsley. I would also add that the Buccaneer solution would have done very little for the industrial aspirations of UK Ltd. There would have been little in it for Rolls-Royce - would you have got a three-spool reheated turbo fan? - and very little for BAe.

Peter Hearne. There would certainly have been something it for the avionics industry. In fact, the radar which was proposed for the Tornado came out of the Buccaneer 2* study. We actually did about nine month's work with a team at Blackburns on a total avionics suite for the Buccaneer, which would have been at least as capable as the Tornado package.

AVM Peter Harding. In 1983 I commanded the first operational Tornado station and my question is really addressed to Dr Lewis. I remember one dark night over East Anglia when, following a total electrics failure, with the back-up electrical systems going as well, both engines subsequently accelerated away to destruction. Electrical failures in the early days of the Tornado were fairly common and the blue flash that accompanied the destruction was pretty disheartening. How did we come to design engines which self-destructed following an electrical failure? Is that the same now or has something been modified?

Dr Gordon Lewis. (*Dr Lewis acknowledged that he was the appropriate member of the panel to field this question but he declined to offer an answer until he had been able to investigate the incident more fully. As promised, he did provide an answer in due course and what follows reflects his written response.* **Ed**)

With the help of Rolls-Royce and my former colleagues I have been able to study the relevant papers and can now offer a considered response to Peter Harding's question. I should make it clear, however, that, notwithstanding the assistance I have received, the views expressed here are mine alone.

The RAF Accident Report, which I have seen, sets out the facts relating to the loss of Tornado GR 1, ZA586, at the end of a night high-low-high TACEVAL sortie on 27 September 1983; the pilot was killed. Passing FL170 in the descent an alternator tripped off line followed by complete failure of the entire electrical system. The engines ran up to overspeed, causing turbine blades to fail due to overheating, followed by surging and loss of power. Post crash investigation found no sign of non-containment of the failed turbine blade shrouds. The navigator ejected as control of the aircraft was lost but the pilot did not, it being established that his seat firing handle had not been pulled.

As there had been a simultaneous and complete loss of both AC *and* DC power, the enquiry considered the possibility that the aircraft's battery had not contained sufficient charge to power the essential services bus bar when transformer rectifier output was lost. Among the actions stemming from the enquiry, two were directly relevant to the behaviour of the engines. First, a pre-flight post-engine start battery check was introduced and, secondly, methods of governing engine speed in the event of loss of electrical power to the Main Electrical Control Unit were to be evaluated.

While this accident was *not* caused by engine failure *per se*, the response of the engine control system to a complete electrical failure does call for comment. The original design and certification were predicated on the basis of the extremely low probability of complete failure of the AC supply system. Engine control was DC powered, either from the transformer rectifiers or, in the unlikely event of AC supply failure, from the aircraft's battery. Overspeed governing was separately powered from the DC supply. Complete failure of the AC system *and* concurrent failure of the DC supply from the battery would result in loss of engine control. In this event the options were failure to a full fuel flow condition or to virtually zero fuel flow. The designer had chosen failure to full fuel flow in order to maintain power at take off and/or low altitude, these being more critical situations than the risk of turbine burn out at medium or high altitude.

Actions were taken to enhance the integrity of the electrical systems and, so far as I am aware, no change was called for to the engine control or overspeed protection. It should be noted that the turbine blade failures were shown to be a consequence of overheating, and that the release of blade shrouds as the RPM exceeded 100% resulted in surge and rundown, thereby preventing higher overspeed that could have led to a possible uncontained failure of the compressor or turbine discs. Under the circumstances additional overspeed protection would *not* have contributed to the maintenance of power.

Finally, the loss of electrical power takes with it all instruments, intercom and radio and reduces aircraft control significantly. The decision to eject was inevitable, but the state of the engines was unlikely to have contributed to the pilot's inability to leave the aircraft.

I appreciate that this explanation leaves several issues unresolved but I have tried only to understand the response of the engines to the primary failure of the electrical systems. This did comply with the certification failure analysis.

Bob Fairclough. NATO has always been dominated by the Americans and NAMMA was a NATO organisation. Did the Americans participate in NAMMA or have any influence over it? And, if none, how did you keep them out?

Skingsley. NATO merely provided a legal umbrella under which NAMMA was set up. NATO represented a convenient framework that did not exist elsewhere. It was no more than that.

Alan Thornber. I have nothing substantial to add to that but I am confident that there was no possibility of anything going on within the

NAMMA organisation at Munich being communicated via the NATO loop to the Americans, or to anyone else.

Jack Gordon. I was the General Manager of the Combined Agency, NAMMA and NAMMO, when it was first set up. Perhaps I can answer the last question. The four nations in the Eurofighter programme established an organisation which was very similar to the one which was set up for the Tornado under a clause in the NATO Treaty which allows any members of the organisation to get together and form a little club, a sort of 'Treaty within the Treaty', which allows those nations paying for a programme to run it in their own way without interference from any of the others, provided only that they pay the bills and behave themselves. Thus the Tornado project was able to operate under the direction of NAMMO without any input whatsoever from the United States Government.

Moving on, I have two questions of my own. As Alan Thornber explained, the development phase of the Tornado project was actually run in steps governed by separate MOUs which effectively allowed each nation to withdraw from the project if it failed to pass specific tests. Why was this done? Was it because nobody expected the project to succeed or was there some other sinister reason which I have failed to grasp? The second question is, did this arrangement significantly interfere with the planning and the conduct of the development phase?

Thornber. I'll try the second question first. The sequential structure did not interfere with ongoing activities, certainly not on the industrial side. It did make a great deal of work, but it was not work which we would not have expected to have undertaken anyhow. It also provided tangible milestones which obliged one to produce real, valid data in order to progress to the next stage of the programme. So, while the ability to withdraw might have created some uncertainty in individuals' minds, it also provided the essential discipline that made sure that we got things right and this, in turn, permitted the customers, the nations, to proceed with the programme with confidence.

Stewart. I would offer another comment on the first part of the question, that is, why Governments were allowed to bail out without any penalties? This was only partially the case. In the early stages of the programme the conceptual phases were actually handled by each nation individually financing the work being done within its own country. By the time that we needed to start more substantial development, however, three countries had already dropped out. At this stage, the remaining Governments were preoccupied with the implications of the reduced numbers of aeroplanes within the residual programme. As I outlined during my presentation, this led to a great deal of reshuffling of workshare and the like and this process *did* involve penalties. Under the MOU, it had been agreed that the national share of development and production would be directly related to the number of aircraft each country purchased. There was a penalty clause that said that, having once agreed its share of development (and thus its financial commitment) if a nation subsequently reduced its order it would not necessarily get its money back and that penalty actually had to be imposed on Germany.

Skingsley. What we signally failed to do was to sort these arrangements out at an earlier stage. In effect, and this is merely my personal view, the UK, in both ministerial and senior civil service form, was seen off by the Germans in this programme. At the working level, certainly within OR, we knew full well that there was never any prospect of Germany buying 600 aircraft. We had sufficient contacts and friends within the German organisation to have absolutely no doubts about this. Yet, on the basis of their initial bid, the project was directed from a Headquarters established in Munich. It was a confidence trick, and we hadn't the wit to see it. We had already been seen off by the French on the AFVG project. We were now being seen off by the Germans. The lesson is that you have to devise a method of introducing penalties, acceptable to the Governments concerned, but enforceable at a much earlier stage. I think that Bill Stewart was hinting that the other nations may not have been sufficiently committed to Tornado in the early stages of the project to have been prepared to sign up to a contract that would have involved significant penalties, but I think that that *has* to be the aim if we are going to avoid being taken for another ride in the future.

Heron. I have to tell an amusing tale about our Chairman when he was my wing commander boss in the OR13 office. Twelve years earlier, as a student at Cambridge, he had read modern languages and, during our initial 'airmen meetings' within the Joint Working Group in Munich, which were conducted in English, we spent many hours harmonising the tri-national air staff requirements. Occasionally the German Air Force delegation would call for a short break in the proceedings to allow them to clarify certain parameters and they would move away from the table to discuss their options (in German naturally). The Boss hadn't acknowledged his fluency in the language so he was well aware of their negotiating position and their intentions before they resumed their places at the table. The German delegation were often frustrated to find their arguments being countered and that they were regularly being outmanoeuvred. It was some time before they learned the secret, divulged inadvertently by the Boss when he ordered lunch from a non-English-speaking cook in the office canteen. At his elbow, unobserved, was the chief of the German Air Force delegation who took it in good part, saying, 'Now we understand.'

AVM John Price. In the overall context of the possibility of withdrawal and the impact of that on the project's ever coming to fruition, I draw your attention to what that great Machiavellian politician Denis Healey had to say on the subject. He suggested that, at some stage, each of the participating countries would probably want to cancel the project but that it would never happen that all three would want to do so at the same time. As a result, he was confident that we would eventually get an aeroplane.

Skingsley. I agree entirely, we did get an aeroplane. It was late and it cost more than expected but we did get it. This was in stark contrast to our failure to acquire TSR2 and F-111 so there is much to be said for collaborative projects in that they are far less likely to be cancelled. Nevertheless, I do not think that that invalidates my contention that we were conned over where the Project Headquarters was established. Perhaps there was some sort of ministerial understanding, to which we were not party, over this arrangement but in the absence of any such explanation, it is difficult to avoid the conclusion that we were robbed.

Heron. Two Tornado development aircraft were lost in looping manoeuvres, one with a German pilot near Manching during a demonstration and one over the Irish Sea flown by Russ Pengelly. What were the causes and was there anything in common?

Paul Millett. There was nothing in common. The first was Ludwig Obermeier who was at about 10 000ft preparing for an aerobatic routine. He advised that he intended to descend to commence his practice display and rolled the aircraft on to its back to pull through to low level but he omitted to select combat flap to enhance manoeuvrability. His failure to do so seriously reduced the lift available from the wing and his pull through was relatively gentle until he realised that the aircraft was very low and the aircraft struck the ground during the late stages of the dive recovery. In simple terms he didn't give himself enough height to recover safely to controlled flight at low level.

Russ Pengelly's accident occurred during a series of toss manoeuvres over the Irish Sea in poor visibility with an ill-defined horizon. He flew one manoeuvre successfully and was descending to 300ft amsl to perform a second test when he flew into the sea. He had not switched on his rad alt and there was a known discrepancy in the barometric altimeter because of position error, although he was aware of this. He was speaking to his navigator on the intercom in normal tones at the time of impact so apparently he was in controlled flight. It is assumed that he was unaware of his proximity to the sea due to the 'goldfish bowl' conditions.

Harding. I am not sure which part of the procurement bureaucracy I should be pointing my finger at, but throughout my first three years at Honington we hurt desperately for Tornado spares with 'Christmas Trees' in the hangar and all that that implied. I just hope that this isn't going to happen again with Typhoon and that procurement of spares is being looked into in a more timely fashion.

Skingsley. I think that we may have to ask the industry to comment on that one but there was certainly a great deal written into the requirement, that the simulator should be available before the aircraft entered service, for instance. You can write these things down, of course, but that doesn't necessarily make them happen!

Wragg. I think the reason for the shortfall was that there was an unrealistic demand for spares because the engine had not been developed to a point where its reliability was adequate. This is a point that I have been seeking to make for most of the day. One must start early and run a test programme designed to establish that all of the engine components are performing to an agreed standard. If you simply wake up on a Monday morning and say 'Let's have a Concorde' or 'Let's have a whatever it is' and pour all the money in at once, without having done any substantial preparation, you are simply not going to get it right first time? That, in essence, is what happened with Tornado.

Hearne. There is another, rather more mundane, answer to Peter Harding's question. I believe that I am right in saying that when it should have been ordering spares, the MOD was having one of its periodic slow downs on spending. As a result, nobody would place the necessary orders. I can assure you that Elliotts were desperately seeking orders for spares so that we could minimise the cost by manufacturing them along with the main production batch. But the Finance Branch simply would not place the contracts. So far as the provision of the avionics back up was concerned, that was certainly the root cause of the problem.

CHAIRMAN'S CLOSING REMARKS

Well, that would be a rather depressing note on which to end so I think that I would rather sum up by pointing out that we have had a very successful day during which we have conducted a very comprehensive survey. I would like to end, therefore, by speaking for the customer, and there are quite a lot of us here.

We have heard quite a bit about the shortcomings of the Tornado project. We must not lose sight of the fact, however, that, despite these problems, the project was ultimately a very successful one. At the end of the day, we, the RAF, got a very good aeroplane, indeed an aeroplane that is still a world beater in its class. I cannot speak for the Italians, but I can speak both for the German crews and for our own, at least up to the time that I left the Service, when I say that they all recognised this. The crews liked their aeroplane and it worked well. It was a collaborative project and I think that that is the only way we are ever going to develop combat aircraft in Europe from now on, so we really must learn the lessons taught by Tornado.

What did we get right? What did we get wrong? What could we have done better? It is the answers to those questions that we need to identify and which are, I hope, being taken note of and implemented in the Typhoon project. The Tornado has now been updated. The current service version is the GR Mk 4, and my guess is that it is going to be with us for at least another fifteen years. The Tornado is an aeroplane that has been, and is going to be, very important to the Royal Air Force. What a good thing that it turned out so well!

SUPPLEMENTARY PAPERS
A FOOTNOTE – COULD A DEVELOPED BUCCANEER HAVE FILLED THE BILL?

Peter Hearne

As I mentioned at an earlier seminar, I was guilty of the sin of suggesting to the Director of Naval Air Warfare in 1961 that, since the RAF was getting into the digital age in the TSR2, the RN could get similar benefits by retrofitting their Buccaneers. Although the seed was sown with both the RN and Brough, not much happened at first. However early study work on conventional weapon modes for the TSR2, and early ideas on flexible response, suggested to us at Elliotts, as we then were, that we ought to look at how we could use these new technologies to improve the accuracy of conventional weapon delivery in as wide a range of weather conditions as possible.

With the cancellation of TSR2 this study work speeded up and Elliotts augmented their existing support team at Brough with a very small group of resident senior system engineers. What emerged was a proposal for the now standard type of package for a largish (by mid-1960s standards) digital computer together with a gas-spin gyro IN platform plus improved displays and an element of auto terrain following

However, the 'New Big Thing' was the proposed radar sensor suite which incorporated a dual X and Q Band Forward Looking Radar together with an LLTV (later FLIR) system. The idea was to try to produce a complementary group of data-fused sensors which started with the longer range detection of the X Band radar, switched to the higher definition of the Q Band in the last part of the run in, with a final 'low light' or thermal image for the drop when conditions permitted. It was this same sensor which was put forward jointly by Elliotts and Ferranti for Tornado.

Under Tornado's collaborative rules, this radar suite would undoubtedly have required a longer and costlier development programme than Texas Instruments' re-packaged F-111 system. However, at the anticipated start date for the Buccaneer programme in 1967 we were already seeing encouraging Q Band performance in a Canberra test bed and it is arguable that a single-nation development programme would have achieved at least equivalent time scales for a Buccaneer 2* IOC.

Although Brough had dreams of afterburning Mach 1.7 supersonic Buccaneer Mk 3$^1/_2$ versions, it seemed to us, as simple minded system engineers, that this new system package in a minimum-change Mk 2 airframe represented the most cost effective solution. It would have produced a major improvement in all-weather attack capability at an earlier date whilst retaining the Buccaneer's penetration speed and the advantages of its significantly greater radius of action, points which were brought out in the symposium. It would have retained a big cold-thrust by-pass engine which could have been augmented for take off, either by water injection or, if and when growth was required, by later Spey variants. This seemed a far surer bet than venturing into the world of re-heat, variable intakes and thin wings. All in all it seemed to go some little way towards our basic system specification of being able to detect and identify an enemy soldier on a bike on top of a mountain at night in a rainstorm and then knock him off. As Kosovo and Afghanistan have shown, this is a capability that is still to be developed in 2002.

Such changes as were needed to the Buccaneer airframe were principally in the radome and nose bay volumes, which were enlarged and stretched, the avionic cooling system and the rear equipment bay, and, last but not least, the cockpit layouts where we evicted the ergonomic slum from the rear seat and substituted a creditable glass cockpit with two large side-by-side electronic displays. The extensive nature of the system change was such that it was best built into newbuild aircraft, thus avoiding fatigue life limitations, although it would have been possible to retrofit younger existing Mk 2s if one could have put up with the aircraft down time.

One feature was the improvement of the existing rather simple Sidewinder fit of some RN aircraft with a proper radar-range-bracket-and-seeker-circle acquisition display on a greatly improved HUD, based on the one supplied to the A-7D/E programme. In addition to providing a credible self defence capability, this HUD would have greatly improved flight safety, compared with the primitive 'stone age' Strike Sight. The HUD also had its own very capable self-contained weapon aiming and flight director computer facilities, the effectiveness of which were well demonstrated by Skyhawks in action against tanks on the Golan Heights in 1973. As a last ditch attempt to provide an upgrade to the Buccaneer we offered to carry out a contractor-funded installation and trial of the HUD using the existing aircraft sensors, radar, etc on an in-service Mk 2.

Although it would have made a major contribution to improving night low level safety factors by replacing the radar altimeter lights with a 'proper' height director, as well as providing effective low level CCIP weapon aiming without the need for 'pop up', the trial was turned down by OR on the grounds that it might jeopardise the Tornado.

There seems little doubt that a national programme of building, say, 100 or so new airframes with a major attack system upgrade in a minimum change version of the existing Spey-Buccaneer would have been much cheaper than participating in the Tornado programme *and* would have come much closer to meeting the RAF's 'strategic' range requirement outlined in Jock Heron's paper. However, it would have lacked what, in the late 60s, the operators perceived to be the essential characteristic of Mach 2 performance along with the 'must have' feature of variable geometry. I cannot help wondering how often Tornado IDS crews ever fly at very much above Mach 1, and indeed, if ever, at Mach 2. Nor can I help noticing that no nation has built any further expensive variable geometry aeroplanes since the Tornado programme. Plainly, neither the F-15 nor the F-16, two of the most successful of multi-role aircraft, feature variable geometry. Fashion, as well as need, appears to have been a powerful driver within the Tornado programme.

An understandable criticism of the Buccaneer 2* proposal is that, while it would been cheaper, it would not have been a 'collaborative' programme and it would thus have lacked the protection against cancellation conferred by the inability of a number of national partners to reach a simultaneous and unanimous decision to chop the programme! As pointed out at the symposium, the future development of military systems seems ever more likely to be of a collaborative nature, so ways must be developed to achieve this in a cost effective manner. The JSF contract will be an interesting 'proof of concept' experience.

Above all, we must get out of the Alice Through The Looking Glass philosophy of preferring to do the *right* thing (ie developing the weapon) in the *wrong* manner (ie via an inefficient, flawed collaborative management structure) because we, as a nation, are unable to order our national defence procurements in a rational long-term manner

These comments are not meant to dispute the main findings of the seminar, namely that the industrial companies, the RAF and the other air forces have developed and put into service a successful and effective strike aircraft which has served us very well and still has some fifteen years or so of useful operational life ahead of it.

However, they do suggest that a more probing analysis, rather than the rush to collaboration as 'the only game in town', might have identified a more cost effective solution. This point was touched on by a House of Commons Select Committee when comparing the Tornado *versus* Buccaneer 2* with the outcome of the Anglo-French collaborative helicopter programme.

OBSERVATIONS FROM THE OR COALFACE
Group Captain Jock Heron

On my return from the USA, following an exchange posting with the USAF, I was posted as a Flight Commander to a Lightning squadron at RAF Wattisham in May 1967. During my arrival week I was urgently summoned to the Station Commander's office to be told that my posting to No 29 Sqn was cancelled and that I was to join the MoD OR Branch as a staff officer where my experience was considered to be 'vital' to the success of the AFVG project. With my family living out of suitcases, I was not best pleased to be detached to the Junior Command and Staff School at Ternhill for two months to learn about files and staff work before joining DOR1's staff as OR13a. I was even less pleased when, some four weeks into the course, I learned that the AFVG, the core of Denis Healy's defence policy, had been cancelled. So, when finally I arrived in Whitehall in August 1967 there was no project to which my 'vital' experience could contribute and the cancellation of my flying tour three months earlier seemed even more frustrating!

There was still much do be done, however, and the three of us in the OR13 office, a wing commander and two squadron leaders, set about supporting the policy staff in their attempts to rescue something from the debris of their collapsed planning assumptions. Finally, in the spring of 1968, the procurement staff began the first tentative contact with the F-104 consortium comprising Canada, West Germany, Italy, Belgium and the Netherlands. They had set up a Joint Working Group (JWG) in Munich to study the requirements for the F-104 replacement and I attended the first formal air staff meeting with the JWG which occurred in July 1968. By 1969 the JWG comprised only the Italians, the German Air Force and Navy, and the British. We found that the aspirations of the

German Navy and the RAF had much in common and from time to time we arranged, after duty hours, to meet the German Navy representative, a pilot who had been trained by the Royal Navy to fly Sea Hawks, to discuss common objectives. Apparently the German Navy had wanted to acquire the Buccaneer instead of the F-104 ten years earlier and they were determined that the German Air Force should not be allowed to dictate their replacement for the F-104.

My tour with the USAF from 1965 to 1967 as an instructor on the F-105 was ideal preparation for the tour in OR. The Thunderchief was a very capable radar-equipped, single-seat, single-engined fighter bomber, a veritable 'TSR1', which was being widely used in Vietnam during my tour at Nellis AFB. My American colleagues briefed me on many of the lessons from SE Asia and my experience in the role stood me in good stead in Whitehall. Knowing how to apply these lessons to the MRCA, however, was an intellectual challenge which I found quite daunting when faced by bright civil service academics and experienced staff college graduates who were adept at asking me 'Why I wanted such and such a feature?' My two-month course at Ternhill was no substitute for a year at Bracknell.

During the MRCA's definition phase there were many healthy debates among the three nations, within the RAF and also between OR in the MoD and the Ministry of Technology (which, in broad terms, fulfilled the function of today's Procurement Executive) in an attempt to harmonise details of the staff requirement. Both the Germans and Italians had considerable experience with the F-104 in the tactical fighter and strike roles and many of their views were strongly influenced by that experience. The RAF had no aircraft in that category to provide comparable views so there were a number of internal disagreements between the RAF staffs in the OR and Operations Branches. When I joined the office in 1967 my wing commander boss was an ex V-bomber test pilot who, three years previously, had been selected to be the Service's first TSR2 pilot. Following its cancellation, he was tasked to evaluate the Buccaneer, the F-111 and the Mirage IV as potential replacements. He was still a 'heavies' pilot at heart, although he was receptive to discussion on the wider role and capability of the new concept of operations.

Many of the other staff officers were ex V Force bomber operators, some of whom were navigators whose experience was limited to flying backwards in the dark at 50 000ft and in these aircraft the navigators had no windows, other than in the prone bomb aimer's position. Few of them had any understanding of the needs of the next generation of strike/attack aircraft whose concept of operation was to fly the IP to target run at M0.9 at 200ft using a variety of avionics systems and visual references to navigate and acquire the target in all weather and at night. When I suggested, for example, that the MRCA should have a clear cockpit canopy over both crew members to permit good all round vision for look out and external reference I was accused of failing to give recognition to the need for a darkened environment to allow the navigator to see his electronic displays in bright sunlight. Furthermore, when I endorsed the need for the pilot to have a moving map display in the front cockpit the navigators accused me of having a single-seat mentality and that knowing the aircraft's position was the navigator's job. Fortunately one of our OR navigator colleagues had served on exchange duties with the RN on the Buccaneer so I gained much needed support for my views from him.

I recall many stimulating meetings when my future career seemed to be doomed, such as that on my arrival when my Deputy Director asked what I thought of the AFVG and its UKVG project brother. My response was to highlight two deficiencies, namely that the engines had insufficient thrust and the wings were too small; both criticisms he deemed to be irrelevant! A further example of my crossing swords with my Deputy Director was his demand to know why I had included in the draft requirement the need for a fully retractable flight refuelling probe. He told me to study the emerging defence policy which stated the UK's intention to withdraw from east of Suez and to recognise that in demanding such a feature, which would involve another increase in empty weight, I was prejudicing the performance of an aircraft that would never operate outside the European theatre and which therefore had no need to refuel in flight. He wasn't prepared to discuss my argument that the government couldn't determine where the next war would be fought and that, wherever it was, the aircraft would have to be able to deploy there. His compromise was to direct that provision should be made for a detachable fixed position probe, like that on the Buccaneer.

My reasoning fell on deaf ears but, with the support of my new wing commander boss, an ex-Canberra low level operator, who joined the office just as we had attended the first of the JWG meetings in Munich I was able to draft an acceptable form of words for the staff requirement.

Hence today the Tornado GR has a bulbous probe assembly which is retractable but which is mounted externally along the fuselage and this piece of equipment is exercised regularly as the RAF's Tornados deploy around the world on operations and training. Fortunately, our successors in the OR office either had a more persuasive argument or had more enlightened superiors to listen to their case for this vital piece of equipment, so the Tornado F.3 has a proper, fully retractable probe and it too is used regularly.

On another occasion, early in the MRCA programme, I attended a meeting in the MoD chaired by my Director to decide if the UK MRCA engine requirement should be for a single or twin layout. Despite the early engine problems with their F-104s, the Italians and Germans were content to accept that a single engine would suffice, primarily on the grounds of cost, simplicity and robustness, although it was acknowledged that reliability and redundancy would be valid considerations. The Director's view, which he had *not* conveyed to us before the meeting, was that we should accommodate their preference. There were a number of Mintech staff at the meeting together with industry representatives and no major objections were raised from around the table. The Director pointedly brought me into the discussions by saying, 'Jock, you have wide experience of single engine operations and I am sure you agree with me.' My answer was, 'No Sir, we need two engines, not just for reliability but primarily for battle damage redundancy.' Immediately after the meeting I was given a one-sided interview by the Director and told not to disagree with him in public, despite my protestations that he had asked me for my personal views and I had told him the truth!

I had composed a notice which we had pinned to the wall in the office which read: 'Requirements can change overnight but the hardware can't - a plea for flexibility!' While this dictum influenced our thinking in the office there were further examples of 'interesting' judgements on the part of the establishment, such as the directive that my wing commander boss and I should *not* visit the new Buccaneer and Phantom units at Honington and Coningsby to brief them on the MRCA and to seek their views on the cockpit layout and crew work-sharing principles for the new aircraft in the light of their experience. Our Deputy Director felt that the front line would be ill-informed on the long term needs of the Service and that they would, therefore, be unable to offer any useful observations. Furthermore, he and his colleagues would not accept the need for the MRCA to be capable of dive attacks from medium altitude. Again, MoD dogma ignored the need for flexibility of operation and so the new weapons for the MRCA were designed solely for 'lay down' delivery in a straight and level run at 200 ft or thereabouts and RAF Tornado and Jaguar operations in the Gulf in 1991 were inhibited as a direct result. I found this apparent inflexibility frustrating and indicative of the V-bomber culture which prevailed in Whitehall at the time.

Nevertheless it was an interesting period which taught me much of the ways of the MoD and served as an introduction to industry which was to stand me in good stead almost twenty years later. I spent several hours at meetings with Rolls-Royce both in the MoD and at the Bristol site to define the characteristics of the engine and many hours with BAe at Warton and elsewhere defining the cockpit and concept of operation for the new aircraft. One of my final tasks was to approve the shape of a model of the MRCA which was to be displayed at the 1970 Farnborough air show where we wanted to present the general arrangement of the aircraft to the public without giving away details of its operational performance, which was still classified. A duplicate of that model is one of our artefacts in the Rolls-Royce Heritage Trust in Bristol today.

The content of the MRCA seminar inevitably concentrated on the design and development of the airframe, engines and avionics. As is usually the case, only passing references were made to other forms of 'equipment' but the many devices that are embraced within this term were quite crucial to the success of the project; they were the humble ha'porths of tar without which the project would most certainly have sunk. Two short papers were subsequently received that serve to highlight the sort of ancillary activity that permits high-technology machines, like variable-sweep aeroplanes, to function. Being relatively unglamorous, however, the sort of problem solving and precision engineering that is involved attracts very little publicity and what there is tends to be lost in the noise generated by the prime contractors. Perhaps these contributions will serve to restore a little of the balance. **Ed**

AIR DENSITY MEASUREMENT TRANSDUCERS FOR TORNADO

Talbot K Green

The story starts with Bloodhound, when Solartron Engineering received a contract to manufacture, under licence, a Swedish gadget which measured air pressure. It was essentially a tin can, that is to say, an enclosed cylinder made from Nispan-C, within which were a couple of coils mounted so as to be mutually perpendicular.

If an AC signal is passed through the first coil, the second detects nothing. But the first coil's electromagnetic fields generate eddy currents within the surrounding cylinder and these, in turn, give off their own magnetic fields which the second coil does pick up.

What the Swedish geniuses had discovered was that, if the cylinder is squeezed, the eddy currents change their paths and give off a different frequency to that which is generating them. The change in frequency is a function of pressure. If the air in the cylinder is evacuated, the change in signal equates to ambient atmospheric pressure. The beauty of this is that the measurement is made electromagnetically with NO moving parts at all; the device would work anywhere in the Universe (outside of Black Holes).

When MRCA's missions were being planned, it was clearly going to have to move very fast and very low, through dense air which would be gusty, lumpy and often moving diagonally - under Herr Ulbricht's power lines, for example, perhaps even under Frau Ulbricht's washing line. To do this the variable geometry air intakes had to be able to adjust independently, and very rapidly, to conditions on either side of the fuselage. With the high frequencies being fed to our little coils, detecting pressure changes and sending instructions to the servos looked relatively easy. Microtecnica simply had to sort out how to do it.

We were tapped on the shoulder and advised that Solartron should take an interest in getting this contract as part of the British share. Our Schlumberger masters said 'OK', and the reliability aspect soon landed on my desk. The theoretical part was an easy application of the current issue of MIL-HDBK-217: after all, there were only the two coils, potted in a block, and four internal and four external joints.

But we were also required to submit field experience of similar products. All I knew was that, in connection with Bloodhound, Solartron had despatched what were known as 'Flygmotors' (from the Swedish owners of the original patent) to (presumably) Filton, after which we had heard no more and we were forbidden by the Official Secrets Act from asking. So I talked to our Electrical Inspection Directorate man who said that he would try to find me a suitable contact. He turned out to be only a mile away, at the RAE, but, while he was very keen to help, there was some embarrassment because, 'We have only a few hours' actual flight experience on Bloodhound and all I can say definitely is that there's no sign in my records that your Flygmotors have ever led to a failure.'

I explained to my boss, John Wood, the Quality Manager, that I could hardly build a very convincing case on that, and we, of course, wanted a steamroller one. Wood was renowned for lateral thinking and pointed out that the technology was not very different from that used in the gas density transducers Solartron made for British Gas. He suggested that I should try to find out how much experience had been built up at Bacton, where North Sea gas came ashore. I knew that Bacton had been using our devices for years and that only one had ever been rejected. British Gas agreed to go through their records which reflected hundreds of thousands of running hours.

Even making adjustments for the rather different operating environments, the fact we had a virtually zero failure rate meant that I still came up with MTBF and Confidence Limit numbers which were well in excess of what the specification called for. So I was able to send my colleague, Robin Baker, off to join the presentation team at Microtecnica with a very strong Reliability Case. We got the contract.

CALIBRATION OF PRESSURE SENSORS
Robin J Baker

Solartron Engineering manufactured pressure sensors used on the Tornado for the derivation of speed and height, and for the control of the engine inlet doors. Their manufacture was an established process but the calibration of production sensors presented a problem. The customer requirement was a calibration curve with the errors not to exceed 0.015% of a reading. So the first problem was to find test gear better, in theory, by an order of magnitude. The only equipment available at the time was a dead weight tester (DWT) that was guaranteed at 0.015% of reading when a compensatory calculation was carried out for each measurement using the vacuum measurement in the bowl and the temperature of the piston/cylinder assembly. The vacuum value was required to compensate for the applied pressure and to allow for the effects of buoyancy. As it is difficult to repeat the same values of vacuum and temperature, and the piston had to be at the same height each time (the difference in height gives a variation in the length of the column of air, hence a different applied weight), a definitive pressure could not be repeated - and how does one measure temperature in a vacuum anyway? Furthermore, you will appreciate that changing pressure, up or down, results in a temperature change.

The first thing we had to do was to calibrate the available test gear. The only organisation able to calibrate our DWT to the required accuracy, 0.005%, was the National Physical Laboratory (NPL), but they would do this as a regular practice only if our calibration system was approved by, and was part of, the British Calibration Service (BCS). Before NPL could do anything for us, the weights for the DWT had to be known to an accuracy of four decimal places of an ounce. We had, therefore, to talk first to the Weights & Measures organisation. Only then would the NPL be able to compare the effective diameter of our DWT's piston/cylinder assembly with their own. How the NPL arrived at their dimension is a mystery to me; of necessity there has to be clearance between the sides of the piston and cylinder. The assembly is spinning all the time, to reduce the effect of 'stiction', so the device is an air bearing. There is air leakage through the system, the higher the pressure the greater the flow, the greater the pressure drop across the assembly and so on. Because the pressure is generated by a known weight acting on a piston of a known diameter, gravity must be taken into account. Gravity at the NPL is different from that at our production facility. A figure was obtained, courtesy of the Royal Aircraft Establishment, a calculation allowing for the difference in height and location of the sites.

So, after we had set up our laboratory and received our BCS approval, we were able to have a calibrated pressure generator. In setting up the laboratory we wanted to make life easier so we tried to reduce the effective vacuum in the DWT bowl. This was not too difficult. We started with the normal pump and, when the vacuum had been reduced to an acceptable level, a diffusion pump was switched in to remove any remaining air, molecule by molecule. The eventual vacuum was such it had only a third order effect and could thus be ignored. To establish the temperature, we glued a calibrated temperature diode to the outside of the cylinder; the laboratory was temperature controlled, so life was simple!

However, using a DWT for production is a very time consuming business and one which is very difficult, if not impossible, to automate. We therefore needed a transfer standard. We produced a temperature controlled box containing several of our own pressure sensors to be linked with a computer; the sensors were calibrated at monthly intervals. The computer program: controlled the oven temperatures; controlled the pressure generated, monitored by the transfer standard; noted that pressure; noted the temperature of the oven; noted the temperature of the production sensors and the output of the sensors. At the end of the production calibration cycle the computer then produced the calibration curve for each sensor, noting and highlighting any errors. A quality assurance check had been introduced, an additional reading over and above that required for calibration was taken. This data was fed into the calibration curve generator; any error was not to exceed the customer's 0.015% requirement.

In the pre-production phase of the project, the quality check was carried out manually. The equation was a cubic; not too difficult using a hand calculator. One day, however, all of the results from the quality check were miles out, all one way. A rapid investigation revealed that a new state-of-the-art computer had been introduced and that, in re-writing the programme, the instruction to use 'double precision' had been omitted.

As the contract progressed, I noted a drift in the transfer standard boxes. This was not all that unusual, it is, in fact, why we calibrate at regular intervals. But this was cyclic. As near as dammit a four week cycle. What has a four week cycle? The Moon - that pulls the tides around!

The old story of the meeting of the lesbian and the homosexual came to mind, I was not sure who was doing what, to whom with which. What were we really trying to calibrate? Tornado sensors? Test gear? The NPL? Tide tables? I do know that the Tornado has been in service for a number of years without any problems associated with the pressure sensors. We must have done something right!

ROYAL AIR FORCE HISTORICAL SOCIETY

The Royal Air Force has been in existence for over 80 years; the study of its history is deepening, and continues to be the subject of published works of consequence. Fresh attention is being given to the strategic assumptions under which military air power was first created and which largely determined policy and operations in both World Wars, the inter-war period, and in the era of Cold War tension. Material dealing with post-war history is now becoming available under the 30-year rule. These studies are important to academic historians and to the present and future members of the RAF.

The RAF Historical Society was formed in 1986 to provide a focus for interest in the history of the RAF. It does so by providing a setting for lectures and seminars in which those interested in the history of the Service have the opportunity to meet those who participated in the evolution and implementation of policy. The Society believes that these events make an important contribution to the permanent record.

The Society normally holds three lectures or seminars a year in London, with occasional events in other parts of the country. Transcripts of lectures and seminars are published in the Journal of the RAF Historical Society, which is distributed free of charge to members. Individual membership is open to all with an interest in RAF history, whether or not they were in the Service. Although the Society has the approval of the Air Force Board, it is entirely self-financing.

Membership of the Society costs £15 per annum and further details may be obtained from the Membership Secretary, Dr Jack Dunham, Silverhill House, Coombe, Wotton-under-Edge, Gloucestershire. GL12 7ND. (Tel 01453-843362)

SECRETARY
Gp Capt K J Dearman
1 Park Close
Middleton Stoney
Oxon
OX25 4AS
Tel: 01869 343327

MEMBERSHIP SECRETARY
(who also deals with sales of publications)
Dr J Dunham
Silverhill House
Coombe
Wotton-under-Edge
Glos
GL12 7ND
Tel: 01453 843362

TREASURER
John Boyes TD CA
5 Queen's Close
Stansted
Essex
CM24 8EJ
Tel: 01279 814225

EDITOR and PUBLICATIONS MANAGER
Wg Cdr C G Jefford MBE BA
Walnuts
Lower Road
Postcombe
Thame
OX9 7DU
Tel: 01844 281449